standard grade study-mate

Muir Johnstone

- a handbook of sources, practice questions and practical advice

history

second edition

Hamilton Publishing

standard grade study-mate

history second edition

First published 1990
Second Edition 1995
© Muir Johnstone 1990, 1995

ISBN 0 946164 18 5 2nd edition
(ISBN 0 946164 11 8 1st edition)

All rights reserved. No part of this publication may be reproduced, stored in a retrieval system, or transmitted, in any form or by any means, electronic, mechanical, photocopying, recording or otherwise, without prior written permission from the publisher.

A catalogue record for this book is available from the British Library.

Orders can be made direct over the phone
Contact Thomson Litho, Hamilton Publishing (Sales)
on (013352) 33081

Access and Visa Cards accepted

Letter accepted with school or personal cheque

Published by
Hamilton Publishing
A division of M & A Thomson Litho Limited
10–16 Colvilles Place, Kelvin Industrial Estate,
East Kilbride G75 0SN

Printed and bound in Great Britain by
M & A Thomson Litho Ltd., East Kilbride, Scotland

CONTENTS

· CHAPTER · ONE ·
EVIDENCE IN HISTORY

Historical Sources	Primary Sources	1–4
Looking at historical evidence	Secondary Sources	4–5
	Using the Evidence	5
Working with Sources	Obtaining Information	6
Handling historical evidence	Building Knowledge and Understanding	6
	Source Setting	7
	Evaluating Sources	7
	Assessing the Reliability of Sources	7–8
Historical Evaluation	The 'How' of History	9–10
Looking at history	Cause: The 'Why' of History	10–11
	Effect: Consequence in History	11–12
	Making Balanced Judgments	13–14

· CHAPTER · TWO ·
INVESTIGATING

Planning the Investigation	16–17
Conducting the Investigation	17
Presenting the Investigation	17–18

CHAPTER · THREE

PRACTICE SECTION

Introduction   19

UNIT 1
- CONTEXT A   Changing Scotland/Britain, 1750s–1850s   20–26
- CONTEXT B   Changing Scotland/Britain, 1830s–1930s   27–35
- CONTEXT C   Changing Scotland/Britain, 1880s–present   36–44

UNIT 2
- CONTEXT A   International Cooperation & Conflict, 1790s–1820s   45–46
- CONTEXT B   International Cooperation & Conflict, 1890s–1920s   47–56
- CONTEXT C   International Cooperation & Conflict, 1930s–1960s   57–65

UNIT 3
- CONTEXT A   People and Power: USA 1850–80   66–69
- CONTEXT B   People and Power: India 1917–47   70–71
- CONTEXT C   People and Power: Russia 1914–41   72–79
- CONTEXT D   People and Power: Germany 1918–39   80–87

APPENDIX A
Specimen Answers

88–99

APPENDIX B
Glossary

100–105

Acknowledgments

106

INTRODUCTION

Your success in Standard Grade History depends upon mastering the skills of historical study as well as demonstrating your knowledge of the past. This book is intended as a complete practical guide to the historical study skills you will be expected to demonstrate in the Standard Grade exam.

All historical study is based upon the use of evidence. CHAPTERS 1 and 2 describe different types of historical evidence and where such evidence might be found. They go on to explain the skills you will need in order to understand, interpret and *investigate* the past: the skills of historical study which will be tested in the exam.

CHAPTER 3 provides you with lots of practice questions to give you experience of handling a broad range of types of historical evidence and to provide plenty of practice in the skills of historical study. Questions from all possible Standard Grade study areas are included. The questions in each exercise are similar to those you will tackle in the Standard Grade exam, helping you to become familiar with the type of question you will be faced with at that important time.

To help you in the practical exercises, in APPENDIX 1 you will find some specimen answers with hints on exam technique and useful notes on what will be expected of you in the examination. Additional help is provided in the GLOSSARY at the end of the book. If you don't understand any word or phrase used in the text, try the Glossary: it may be explained there.

You will gain most benefit from the guide by seeking the expert assistance and advice of your class teacher as you progress. Once familiar with the book you might find that the early section on historical evidence will be most useful as something to dip into; the historical skills breakdown and the practice exercises are intended as practical working sections. *Best of luck!*

MJ

CHAPTER · ONE ·
EVIDENCE IN HISTORY

HISTORICAL SOURCES

In finding out about the past, historians make use of items of evidence. These items are usually called historical sources. The value of a particular source depends upon its usefulness in providing information which adds to our knowledge and understanding of past times.

PRIMARY SOURCES

These provide us with some form of first-hand or direct evidence of something that happened in the past. The series of primary sources which follows shows aspects of twentieth-century working-class life.

▶ **SOURCE 1**   *An observer writing about London's unemployed, 1903:*

A living picture of misery... the processions of unemployed which paraded our main streets. One afternoon alone I counted over four thousand men. The keen air and searching wind made the day trying even to the well-fed and well-clad. Many were lads, and some were very old men. Stunted beings barely five feet high, with white faces and pigeon breasts, marched by burly porters. Few had overcoats, and it was not always wise to look below the tightly buttoned jackets for vests.

Eye-witness accounts are the most direct form of primary source evidence. The above account, written by a person trained carefully to observe living conditions among poor people, describes unemployed dock-workers in London's East End.

Of course, such eye-witness accounts are not only found in written sources. *Oral evidence* is spoken evidence from or about past times. This is often used to help bring alive past situations and events. You might find that you yourself can make use of taped interviews with people who have special memories of the past: perhaps in your historical investigation you may even choose to carry out your own interviews to add to your knowledge and understanding of the topic you are exploring.

Another sort of eye-witness is the camera. *Photographs* provide us with first-hand visual accounts of the past. *Paintings, engravings* (pictures cut in metal, wood, etc. for the purpose of printing), and

▶ **SOURCE 2**   *Slums in London, about 1900.*

drawings are personal eyewitness accounts in that they present us with one person's view of the past. These personal impressions might be very different from the real scene as captured in a photograph. Although care must therefore be taken in using paintings, engravings and drawings as historical evidence, these sources give us interesting, often fascinating, glimpses of the past.

Diaries kept by individuals are sometimes of such historical interest that they have been published as books. Such printed diaries might cover a few weeks or months or might be a lifelong record. *Memoirs* and *recollections* are similar personal memories, often based upon carefully kept diary accounts of the writer's life.

▶ **SOURCE 3**   *Lady Asquith's memories of childhood:*

It was a time of booming trade, of great prosperity and wealth... Dire, grinding poverty still stalked the streets in that hey-day of our prosperity. I can remember as a child being haunted by the beggars in the streets, the crossing-sweepers... the children in rags, fluttering like feathers when the wind blew through them.

Memoirs and recollections are sometimes made up of chance memories, which for some reason stay in the writer's mind. A more ordered set of recollections following the course of the writer's lifetime is usually called an *autobiography*.

Records or reports describing particular past situations or events at the time they happened are often used as historical evidence. Such sources are usually called *contemporary records*. (Contemporary means 'belonging to the same time'.)

▶ **SOURCE 4**   *Report on slum housing, London, 1903:*

NUMBER ONE ALPHA STREET: A young couple with two children at school. The father is a dock labourer who at the beginning of December had been five weeks out of work. The mother is a ragsorter who earns nine shillings a week. They live in one wretchedly dirty room, with scarcely any fire or food, and they pay three shillings a week rent.

Contemporary records come in many different forms. This example is from a survey of living conditions among London's urban poor.

There are many different kinds of contemporary record. Among the most commonly used are official reports and records made for or by national and local government bodies. In looking at particular aspects of the past — for instance nineteenth-century working conditions in mines and factories, or public health in Britain's towns and cities — you could make use of the Reports of Government and Royal Commissions of Enquiry set up to examine and report on these things.

Such public records might be held by National and Local Public Records Offices. Another useful source might be Local Registry Offices (births, marriages and deaths records). For even older records it is worth checking local Parish Records. Perhaps your local library might hold Local Census Records which will give you details of the population in your area in the past (earliest census records are for the year 1801). These are now sometimes transferred on to computer database files. If they are available in this handy form, your teacher might be able to help you obtain the Census disks and arrange for use of school computer systems. Ask your teacher which of these sources would be most useful to you in your Investigation (see Chapter 2) and how you should go about finding them.

Publications like *newspapers* and *magazines* often give us fascinating glimpses of past times. Contemporary news stories not only tell us the facts of a story as it occurred, but also show us what ordinary people thought of their own times and often tell us much about the day-to-day life of the community in which they lived.

Non-news items in the newspaper, from 'letters to the editor' to 'situations vacant' (jobs on offer) and 'articles for sale' give us clues to public tastes and values, political opinion, leisure and other interests of the time.

▶ **SOURCE 5**   *Newspaper extracts (as shown opposite).*

There are of course different kinds of newspapers: some deal with national, some with local news; there are daily and weekly papers, and magazines issued less often than that. Most newspapers and magazines aim at interesting and even entertaining their readers as well as informing them. National newspapers often have their own definite viewpoint on current affairs. For example, a newspaper might be for or against the government of the day, and this can give a clear bias or 'slant' to their coverage of news stories. The historian must be alert to such matters when using newspapers and magazines as historical sources.

Newspaper and magazine *cartoons* often make some comment upon individuals, events and developments of the time. The political cartoon is the most common of all.

▶ **SOURCE 6**   *Cartoon from* Punch *magazine, 1909.*

RICH FARE
'Fee, fi, fo, fat
I smell the blood
of a plutocrat
Be he alive, or be he dead
I'll grind his bones
to make my bread'

Newspaper extracts as a source

▶ SOURCE 7 *A poster of 1931.*

You must always use your own knowledge of the topic on which the cartoonist is commenting. In the example shown the figure with the club represents David Lloyd George, Chancellor of the Exchequer in the Liberal Government which introduced old age pensions and other welfare changes between 1905 and 1911. In 1909 he brought in a Budget which aimed at raising £16,000,000 from higher taxes to pay for the new social welfare schemes. Increases in income tax meant that the rich and politically powerful upper class (represented by the cowering 'plutocrat' in the cartoon) had to pay much more in 'supertax' and in bigger taxes on business profits.

As you no doubt can see from this example, political cartoons can be difficult to understand. Your teacher's help will be needed here. As you build your knowledge and understanding, however, you will find it easier to grasp the meaning of contemporary cartoons, and hence make use of them as evidence in your historical studies.

In your studies you will come across a wide range of *posters* and public notices. The purpose of the poster might simply be to give information. Some posters might have a different aim: political posters and some wartime posters for instance attempted to sway public opinion by putting a case for a particular viewpoint or argument.

As with the political cartoon discussed earlier, you must use your own knowledge of the topic dealt with in the poster. The aim of the poster above was to persuade people to vote for the National Government in the General Election of 1931. The National Government included members from all three main political parties — Labour, Conservative and Liberal. The poster argues that such a government was needed in order to deal successfully with the massive problems caused by the financial 'crash', business slump and mass unemployment of the early 1930s.

This source is deliberately one-sided because it gives a view of things which supports the National Government. Deliberately biased sources like this are called *propaganda*. The purpose of propaganda is to persuade: because of this, sources such as political and war posters need to be examined carefully if used as historical evidence. In fact one possible interest in looking at such sources is to examine the nature and type of in-built bias or one-sidedness in the propaganda and what this tells us about its authors, and their aims.

In studying the history of the last 100 years or so, the historian can make use of 'stills' photographs like the example shown in Source 2. Sometimes movie film can be used.

Newsreel film provides pictures and spoken reports on news items of the time. The spoken reports are usually in the form of a 'voice-over' commentary giving the background to each newsreel item. Newsreel commentary is often clearly biased, presenting a particular viewpoint on the news. In particular wartime newsreel usually contains obvious propaganda against enemy nations. As with propaganda posters discussed earlier, newsreel sources must be examined carefully, so that fact can be separated from opinion. On the other hand, again as noted earlier, if the object is to examine the nature of the propaganda itself, then this kind of historical source is extremely useful to the history student.

Documentary film, describing aspects of life at particular times and in particular societies, is always of value to the historian. Usually documentary films are less likely to have clear propaganda purposes, but this cannot be taken for granted. As with all types of historical evidence, the historian must proceed with care and be alert to the possibility of perhaps less obvious bias. In a few cases documentaries are, however, clearly intended as propaganda. The newsreel-type coverage of the 1936 German Olympic Games by Leni Riefenstahl or the documentary reconstruction of the 1917 Russian Bolshevik October Revolution by Eisenstein are examples of this.

Films made for the *movie cinema* — from the early days of Hollywood silent melodramas, epics and comedies through to the movies of our own times — are a valuable historical resource. These often provide a colourful commentary on the life and times of the society and the culture from which they sprang.

One of the most enjoyable ways of learning about the past is through examination and investigation of artefacts (manufactured articles) belonging to the historical period you are studying. These are called *historical artefacts*. The value of old photographs, paintings, engravings and drawings in bringing alive the past has already been noted. In addition to these, national and local museums and some libraries and resource centres maintain historical period collections which might contain artefacts, large and small, from our common historical past. Heritage museums and museum parks provide sites in which larger artefacts such as factories, mines and machines can be examined.

Last but not at all least, your own local village, town or city, and its buildings, monuments, and streets, is a historical archive often providing useful, interesting evidence of earlier times.

SECONDARY SOURCES

Generally a secondary source is an account of the past given by someone with a special interest in the events described. This individual might be a historian or a writer with particular knowledge of the period or situations involved. Memoirs and autobiographies written a long time after the events they describe took place are really more like secondary than primary sources, since the author has the benefit of hindsight — of looking back on events — in creating his or her account.

The commonest type of secondary source you will deal with is the history textbook or topicbook. In addition to describing events, situations and developments of the past, these books often attempt to explain or comment upon aspects of the historical period or topic with which they are dealing.

Secondary sources need not always be books however: an article in a magazine or newspaper, a recorded talk, a film or video describing or discussing a historical topic or period, slides or filmstrip materials — all these can be secondary source works. You will be able to use many such sources. They will provide a useful guide to your historical studies and help you think your way through the past.

Books, articles, talks or film and video programmes about the past are based upon the writer's understanding of the topics covered. This understanding is itself based upon knowledge of primary sources relating to these topics. Sometimes extracts from these primary sources are included in the secondary work. Try to examine how the author makes use of these primary sources; the ways in which they further his or her understanding of the past. Your own grasp of the topic under study will improve as you do this. The exercise will also help you — as historian — to see how historical study can be organised and carried out.

The table below summarises what you have just learned about historical sources.

Summary: Historical Sources

Primary sources

- Provide first-hand evidence of the past

- Appear in a variety of forms:
  Eye-witness accounts
  Photographs
  Paintings, drawings, engravings
  Diaries, memoirs, autobiographies
  Contemporary records
  Newspapers and magazines
  Cartoons and posters
  Contemporary film
  Historical artefacts

Secondary sources

- Give an account of the past from an interested individual

- Usually include explanation and analysis as well as description

- Are based upon examination of relevant primary sources

- Provide a guide to progress through the topic

- Provide an example of the historical study process

USING THE EVIDENCE

When you are using a historical source always begin by asking a number of general questions. The purpose of this is to help you ensure that you understand the nature and overall content of the source. The checklist which follows shows you the kind of questions which will help you achieve this aim.

Getting to know a source: a questions checklist

Instruction: *Read over the source once; ask the questions below.*

Source Identification

Origin	When did the source first appear? Where and in what circumstances did it first appear?
Author	Is there a source author? Can the author be identified?
Nature	What is the nature of the source (e.g. eye-witness account, photograph, memoir, contemporary record, etc.)?

Placing the Source

Actuality	Is the source complete or incomplete? Do we know if it has been altered or rearranged in any way?
Purpose	Did the source have any particular purpose? Can we describe this purpose?
Significance	Did (does) the source have any special significance? Can we describe or explain this significance?

Instruction: *Read the source more carefully; ask the questions below.*

Language	Can you follow the written text?
Terminology	Are there particular words or phrases you don't understand?
Ideas	Are there particular ideas you find difficult to grasp?
Background	Are there references to things outside the source which need to be followed up in order to understand the source? Is there any new knowledge you need to acquire before working with the source?

Jot down any doubts or problems you have as you make your way through the checklist. *Ask your teacher's help if required.* If you find it useful, make up a checklist like the one shown. Remember that in your Investigation (see Chapter 2) you will be selecting your own sources. In this case you might find the completed checklist has extra usefulness as an information guide which you can file away and re-use if you need to check back on your sources.

WORKING WITH SOURCES
OBTAINING INFORMATION

All historical sources provide information about the past. This information can be used to build knowledge about people, events, situations and developments of past times. Having looked carefully at your particular source and asked some general questions about it (see previous page), look at the details contained in the source. Try to select important and useful information and extract this from the source.

Look at the source below. It is from a Parliamentary Report on Railway Transport and dates from the year 1844.

Comparative costs

	£	s	d
By Canal Boat, Manchester to London			
Two adults' passage, fourteen shillings each	1	8	0
Three children's passage, seven shillings each	1	1	0
Provisions, etc. for five days passage	1	5	0
Total	3	14	0

	£	s	d
By Coach, Manchester to London (186 miles)			
Two adults' passage, thirty shillings each	3	0	0
Three children's passage, fifteen shillings each	2	5	0
Coachman and Guard		7	0
Food, etc.		10	0
Total	6	2	0

	£	s	d
By Railway, Manchester to London (212 miles)			
Third-class, Manchester to Birmingham			
Two adults' passage, eleven shillings each	1	2	0
Three children's passage, five shillings and sixpence each		16	6
Third-class, Birmingham to London			
Two adults' passage, fourteen shillings each	1	8	0
Three children's passage, seven shillings each	1	1	0
Food, etc., one shilling and sixpence each		7	6
Total	4	15	0

Obtaining information: What does the source tell us about:

> Forms of transport which could be used in 1844?
>
> What people using each form of transport had to pay for?
>
> How the prices varied between different forms of transport?

There are many examples of questions calling for selection of information in the Practice Section of this book.

In the example shown above only one source is used. Sometimes you will need to use more than one and you might need to compare and cross-refer between sources to obtain or check information. This can sometimes be a little complicated, so ask your teacher's help if you need to.

BUILDING KNOWLEDGE AND UNDERSTANDING

Obtaining information is the first step in learning about the past. We can only claim knowledge however when we understand the importance of the information obtained from the source(s) and can make use of this to improve our understanding of past events, situations or developments.

The source on the left clearly provides us with information on transport costs in 1844. If we are to make use of this information in learning about mid-nineteenth-century transport in Britain, we need to use the source to answer important questions about the topic itself.

Look again at the source *Comparative costs*, 1844. Try to answer the following questions:

> Why do costs for food and other items vary for different forms of transport?
>
> If you were an adult planning to take your family on a journey from Manchester to London in 1844, what advantages and disadvantages would you see in using each form of transport?

The question which follows calls for additional understanding. You are being asked to apply knowledge gained from the source about one aspect (passenger transport) to comment on another aspect (commercial transport).

> The source deals only with passenger costs. If you were a Lancashire cotton manufacturer sending rolls of cotton cloth from Manchester to a London warehouse, how would you decide which form of transport to use?

If you had already studied transport changes during the Industrial Revolution, you could attempt a broader question.

Using your knowledge of the topic, answer the following questions:

> What advantages and disadvantages did canals and roads have as means of transporting goods and people in mid-nineteenth-century Britain?
>
> How did the growth of industries affect transport in nineteenth-century Britain?
>
> Why is the name the 'Railway Age' sometimes given to this period of British history?

SOURCE SETTING

So far the study exercises we have looked at have shown how to obtain information from historical sources and how to use this to test and improve our understanding of the past.

We can never assume however that information from a particular source is unquestionably truthful and accurate. Sources can be intentionally or unintentionally misleading, inaccurate or simply and plainly wrong. It is the historian's task not only to extract information from sources, but also to try to assess the accuracy of the information obtained.

This is often a difficult task, requiring care and cleverness. Sometimes the historian has to play detective; the nature of the source, and the motives and intention of the source's author(s) need to be looked at as closely as the source itself.

By carrying out the general questioning exercise outlined earlier (see page 5), you will have examined such things as the origin, authorship, nature and possible purpose of the source.

Next, try to set the source in its own historical time and place — in its own historical setting or context as this is often called.

Look at the source 'Factory Work' shown below.

Consider the following source setting questions:

- What tells us that the source is dealing with Britain during the time of the first Industrial Revolution?

- What does the source tell us about industry at this particular time in the past?

- Why might the source be of particular interest to a historian studying this period in Britain's past?

EVALUATING SOURCES

Having set a source in its historical context, we should next ask why and in what ways the source is of value in informing us about the past.

Sometimes the value lies in the source's usefulness in bringing alive the past.

We noted before that a source which presents an obviously biased (one-sided) view of things, might be of value to the historian because it helps us to understand more clearly the opinions and attitudes of those who held this view.

Look at this election poster of 1910. (Keir Hardie was Labour Party candidate in Merthyr constituency). Look also at the engraving 'Over London by Rail' on page 8.

We could learn about how Central London looked in the 1870s, and about Labour Party aims in 1910, from many secondary textbooks. What then is the particular value of the sources shown in informing us about these subjects?

ASSESSING THE RELIABILITY OF SOURCES

In trying to assess how accurate or truthful a particular source is, we need to look again at the origin of the source, think of the possible bias of the source's author(s) and try to work out whether the source was designed for a purpose. For instance it may have been designed to persuade others to accept the opinions or views of the source's author(s).

Over London by Rail (Gustav Doré, 1872)

SUSPICIOUS LOOKING PARTY
'Any objection to my company, Guv'nor?
I'm agoin' your way' (aside) 'and further'

Look again at the 1910 election poster (on page 7) and at the cartoon shown here (from *Punch* magazine, 1909).
Think of the following question:

> How reliable are the sources as descriptions of British socialism at this time?

To answer the question, we would need to:

- place each source in its historical time and place (to ensure understanding).

- look at the purpose, nature and authorship of each source and think how these might have affected the source (see the paragraph at the bottom of page 7).

- look for possible bias, exaggeration, inaccuracy in each source.

- try to work out the impression of British socialism given in each source.

- make a final assessment of reliability based upon these things.

HISTORICAL EVALUATION

THE 'HOW' OF HISTORY

In trying to judge how useful a source is in giving us information about the past, and attempting to assess the accuracy and truthfulness of this information, we need to look ever more closely at the source. Only through careful, intelligent questioning of the historical evidence which the source presents can we hope to get at or near the historical truth.

Look at the two sources below.

Ascent of Montgolfier Balloon from M. Revillor's garden, 1783

You can easily provide answers to the basic questions:

What is happening? When and where? Who was involved?

What about the question **'how'**?

How did methods of achieving human flight change between 1790 and 1903?

You would mention of course that balloons gave way to more solid constructions; that wings took the place of lighter-than-air gas; that powered forward motion essential to take-off in heavier-than-air machines was provided by petrol-driven motors and screw propellers.

This is a fairly straightforward example of a historical **'how'** question, because it can be answered by comparing two items of evidence. Other types of **'how'** question are not quite so straightforward however. Look at the example below.

> How did Britain become involved in the First World War?

You might begin to examine this question in the following way:

- *Look at the question carefully:* **'How'** *here means* **'in what way'**.
- *Make sure you know the background facts: when Britain went to war; who made the declaration of war; where this occurred etc.*

First 'heavier-than-air' flight of the Wright brothers, Kitty Hawk, Carolina, 1903

- *The first sensible step is to read over the section of a familiar textbook which deals with Britain's entry into the First World War. If you have covered this topic in class, read over your course notes.*

Here are three sources dealing with the topic.

▶ **SOURCE A** *From a speech by Sir Edward Grey, British Foreign Secretary, House of Commons, 3 August 1914:*

The present crisis originated in a dispute between Austria and Serbia ... The Government of France are involved in it because of their alliance with Russia ... We are not parties to the Franco-Russian alliance ... I now come to what we think the situation requires of us ...

We have got the consideration of Belgium which prevents us from any unconditional neutrality and we are bound not to shrink from proceeding to the use of all the forces in our power.

▶ **SOURCE B** *From a secondary text:*

At 10.30 am on 4th August 1914 the King, attended by only one minister and two court officials, sanctioned the proclamation of a state of war with Germany from 11 pm. That was all. The Cabinet played no part once it resolved to defend the neutrality of Belgium. It did not consider the ultimatum which Grey sent (to Germany) after consulting only the Prime Minister ... and perhaps not even him. Parliament, though informed of events, did not give formal approval to the Government's acts.

▶ **SOURCE C** *From a secondary text:*

On 4th August the German armies poured over the Belgian frontier. In Berlin the British Ambassador took a message to the German Chancellor. It said that if the German troops did not leave Belgium before midnight, Britain would declare war on Germany and Austria. The Ambassador, Sir Edward Goschen, knew perfectly well that the Germans could not pull out of Belgium by midnight. By then the British Ambassador and his staff were gone and Britain declared war.

To answer the question:
- *Study the sources: put the primary source (A) in its historical time and place. How useful is the information given by the sources? How accurate is the information likely to be?*
- *A good idea might be to jot down a 'time-line' of events leading to Britain's entry into the war.*
- *Compare the information given in the sources (ie cross-refer sources).*
- *When you feel you have a grasp of the whole question, use your 'events time-line' and source evidence to describe how Britain went to war.*

CAUSE: THE 'WHY' OF HISTORY

A **'how'** question asks for description of some kind. In our previous example, by describing the stages in Britain's entry into the war, we tried to show how Britain became involved in the European conflict. In looking at the past, we must also look at the often more difficult **'why'** questions.

One common type of **'why'** question asks us to explain why things happened as they did. Such a question is asking us to examine historical *cause*.

Let us examine a particular **'why'** question.

> Why did Britain go to war in 1914?

- *Look at the question: **'why'** here means **'for what reasons'**. We need therefore to look for possible British reasons for going to war.*
- *Reasons and motives for countries acting as they did are often complicated and sometimes difficult to search out. As we noted before, the best first step is to read over sections of a familiar textbook or your own course notes dealing with the topic.*
- *Some of the sources shown for the earlier **'how'** question on Britain's entry into the war are again of use in answering our **'why'** question.*

Look again at the sources A, B and C above. Some additional sources follow giving useful information for the **'why'** question.

▶ **SOURCE A** *Extract from interview with the German Kaiser, published in the* Daily Telegraph, *October 1908:*

I have said time after time that I am a friend of England, and your press bids the people of England refuse my proffered hand and insinuates that the other holds a dagger ... Germany would always keep aloof from politics that would bring her into complications with a sea power like England ... But what, you will say, of the German Navy? Surely that is a menace to England! Against whom but England are my (sea) squadrons being prepared? ... My answer is clear: Germany is a young and growing empire ... She has a world-wide commerce

... Germany must have a powerful fleet to protect that commerce.

▶ **SOURCE B** *From a secondary text:*

On 2nd August 1914 Germany moved into Luxemburg and on the 3rd into Belgium. By the Treaty of London of 1839, both Britain and Prussia (the leading German state at that time) had promised to guarantee Belgian neutrality. If Germany violated it (ie ignored Belgian neutrality) now she would put herself hopelessly in the wrong with every section of British opinion. When the British Ambassador in Berlin stated what Britain's attitude to such an action would be, the German Chancellor inquired whether Britain would plunge into war for the sake of a 'scrap of paper'. But a Belgium under German control meant more than tearing up a 'scrap of paper' to Britain, it meant the danger of a great hostile naval power within easy distance of her shores. For centuries Britain had made the freedom of Belgium from control by a major naval power the main point of her foreign policy.

▶ **SOURCE C** *Extract from the Treaty of London, signed in 1839:*

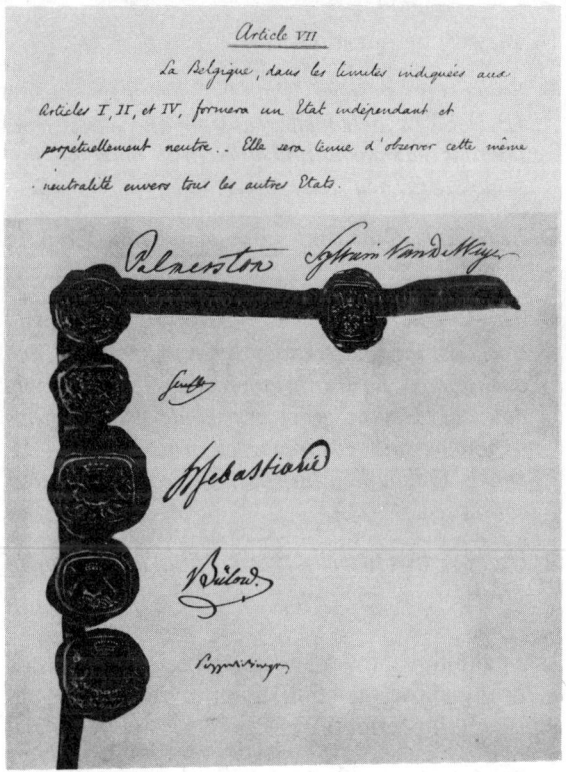

'Belgium ... will form an independent and ... neutral State.'

To answer the question:

- *Study the sources: Put the primary sources (A,C) in their historical time and place. How useful is the information given in all sources? How accurate is the information likely to be?*

- *In this particular case, it might be helpful to make a list or table of possible reasons for Britain's decision to go to war in 1914.*

- *Think carefully about each possible reason: assess its importance in relation to what you have learned and understood about international affairs in the period leading up to the outbreak of war.*

- *Compare the information given in the sources. Are there conflicting or different reasons given for British entry into the war?*

- *When you have completed these exercises you should be able to make your final statement on 'Why Britain went to war in 1914' by listing and explaining Britain's reasons for going to war and giving your view on the importance of each reason as one possible cause of Britain's entry into the war.*

EFFECT: CONSEQUENCE IN HISTORY

The more straightforward type of '**effects**' question asks us to describe the *result* or *effects* of events or developments in the past. In answering the question:

> What military gains and losses resulted from the Somme campaign (1916)?

... you could describe gains and losses of territory during, and as a result of, the Somme campaign, list casualties, loss of equipment and so on.

A more difficult '**effects**' question might ask you not only to describe the results of military campaigns like the Somme, but also to explain the particular importance of these results. The question:

> What effects did large-scale campaigns like the Somme have on the generation which lived through the time of the First World War?

... asks you to describe short-term and longer-term effects of such campaigns on the people — soldiers and civilians — who lived through the war years.

Let us examine a particular '**effects**' question:

> What were the effects of war on Germany's civilian population by 1918?

- *Look at the question: note that it is the effects of war on civilians in Germany in the last year of war, 1918, which are asked for.*
- *Knowledge of Germany's home-front during the First World War is required background information. Begin by looking at the section(s) of a familiar textbook dealing with the German home-front between 1914 and 1918, or look over your course notes if you have covered the topic in class.*

Here are examples of sources giving information about the topic.

▶ **SOURCE A**   *Adapted from a secondary text:*

The mood of the nation was gradually changing. The miseries and bereavements affected the mass of the civilian population. A shortage of labour, horses and fertilisers was damaging the productivity of German farmers ... Urban workers were especially badly affected by food shortages and their discontent showed itself in occasional riots.

▶ **SOURCE B**   *German emergency soup kitchen, 1918.*

▶ **SOURCE C**   *From a secondary text:*

The population was war-weary and starving. Thousands were dying of a new menace, Spanish Influenza, mainly because their resistance to disease was weakened as a result of prolonged starvation. Riots and revolutions began to break out in the major cities. Deserters from the war front swelled the angry mobs.

▶ **SOURCE D**   *Two comments, 1918:*

Austrian minister to German Kaiser: If the monarchs of the Central Powers are not able to conclude peace during the next few months, the peoples will go over their heads and the waves of revolution will sweep away everything for which our brothers and sons are still fighting and dying.

German 'Freikorps' recruiting poster:
Inside the Reich chaos is mounting
Plunder and disorder are everywhere.
Nowhere can one find respect for law and justice or respect for personal and government property.

▶ **SOURCE E**   *Armed civilians, Germany, 1918.*

To answer the question:
- *Study the sources: Put the primary sources (B,D,E) in their historical time and place. How useful is the information given in all sources? How accurate is each source likely to be?*
- *List effects of the continuing war on the German people.*
- *Think of how you wish to arrange your list: you could list the effects under different headings such as shortages, hardship, growing discontent, breakdown of law and order; you could list the effects chronologically (in the order in which they happened) to show how the effects increased as the war continued.*
- *Use your lists to write out your final description of effects.*

As an additional exercise, using the same sources as for the above question, think of how you would approach this **'effects'** question:

   As a German soldier returning home at the end of the war, describe the effects of four years of war on you and your country.

MAKING BALANCED JUDGMENTS

Some questions call upon you to state and explain your own views on events or developments in the past. Here are some examples:

How successful was the British coal industry in making use of new technology in the 1920s and 1930s? Give reasons for your answer.

How important a change was the introduction of voting rights for women in twentieth-century Britain? Explain your answer.

'There is no separate Scottish culture or way of life in twentieth-century Britain.' Do you agree? Explain your view.

Such questions require good knowledge and understanding of the topics involved. In each case you are called upon to make some form of *judgment*. You are also asked to explain your judgment as part of the exercise. You can do this only if your answer shows you have a clear understanding of the topic, and you have thought your way through the question to reach a sensible, balanced judgment.

Let us look at a particular '**judgment**' question:

> 'The Welfare State, the finest creation of post-1945 Britain'. Do you agree with this verdict? Explain your answer.

- *Look at the question: are you sure that you understand what is meant by 'Welfare State'? Note that you must assume that 'post-1945 Britain' means Britain between 1945 and the present.*

- *You must have good knowledge about the origins of the Welfare State and its development since 1945, and must show understanding of its aims, problems and achievements to the present time. Begin by looking at the section(s) of a familiar textbook or your own course notes dealing with the topic.*

Here are sources giving information about the British Welfare State.

▶ **SOURCE A** Daily Mirror, *July 1948*:

THE DAY IS HERE! For years the reformers of all parties have tried to safeguard the aged the poor and the sick. Much has been done . . . But you always wanted fuller protection against misfortune. You wanted the State to accept larger responsibility for the individual citizen who served it faithfully. YOU WANTED SOCIAL SECURITY. FROM THIS DAY HENCE, YOU HAVE IT.

▶ **SOURCE B** *Adapted from a secondary text:*

On the morning of the 'Appointed Day', July 5th, 1948, *The Times* asked: 'Can the next generation reap the benefits of a social service state while avoiding the perils of a Santa Clause (a something-for-nothing) State?'

Many of the older generation would say that the 'perils' have not been avoided. They would very likely claim that today people 'have it too easy' and that having everything 'served up on a plate' takes away initiative and ambition.

▶ **SOURCE C** *Two views of the Welfare State (Punch magazine).*

Land of Promise, 1948

Welfare State, 1949

▶ **SOURCE D** *The* Daily Telegraph, *1976:*

Among the increasing ranks of the unemployed are professional job-dodgers who avoid offers of work so that they can draw dole-money. The majority are men in the 18 to 36 age-group who are idle to the backbone and twice as devious. They boast of the jobs for which they have been rejected and smirk at the stupidity of the social security authorities ... One looked shocked when told his weekly wage would be £50 'Come off it Guv'nor,' he said, 'I'm getting £38 a week off the State for doing nothing!

To answer the question:

● *Study the sources: put primary sources in their historical time and place. How useful is the information given? How accurate is each source likely to be?*

● *Make up a list of arguments 'for' and 'against' the view of the Welfare State put forward in the question.*

● *Think carefully about each argument. Is it realistic? Is it accurate? Does it make a real point?*

● *Try to place the various arguments 'for' and 'against' in what you see as an order of importance.*

● *Write out your final answer to the question, listing all the arguments 'for' and 'against' and explaining how you have compared the importance of these in reaching your balanced judgment.*

CHAPTER·TWO·
INVESTIGATING

All candidates in Standard Grade History must carry out a detailed **Historical Investigation** as part of their course work. This Investigation will involve you in three *activities*:

1 **Planning the Investigation**
2 **Conducting the Investigation**
3 **Presenting the Investigation**

While it is possible for you to work alongside others interested in the same topic, even those looking at similar issues within the topic, you must carry out each of the activities shown above for yourself.

You will be assessed for all three investigative activities. Your work in planning and conducting (carrying out) your Investigation will be assessed by your class teacher as you go along. You must produce a final Report which is assessed at the end of your Investigation.

The Investigation is assessed in this way because History is not just 'knowledge of the past' but is the process or method by which we study the past. When you carry out your Investigation you are setting up your own process for studying your chosen issue, using the basic historical study skills outlined in Chapter 1.

Your teacher will need to examine and, from time to time, talk to you about your work. So *keep a careful record of your progress*. Be prepared to explain *what you have done* and *what you next plan to do* in your Investigation.

While it is important for you to discuss the progress of your work with your teacher, the aims of your Investigation, as well as the sources you select, and the methods of study you use are very much your decisions. It is up to **you** to carry out all the tasks involved.

Planning an Investigation	Select a topic	
	Choose an issue or issues to be investigated	
	Think of questions that need to be examined in looking at the issue(s)	**Look for evidence** which relates to your issue(s) and questions (see pages 1–5)
Conducting an Investigation	Select items of evidence (**Sources**)	**Use historical evidence** to examine the issue(s) involved (see page 5)
	Obtain information from available evidence	**Work with the sources** you have selected (see pages 6–14)
		Make use of as broad a range of evidence as you can locate.
Presenting an Investigation	Present the outcome of the exercise in an appropriate form of Investigation Report	**Decide** on the **form** of the report
		Decide on **layout** of the report
		Make out a rough draft of the report
		Prepare the finished report

INVESTIGATING: A HISTORICAL STUDY EXERCISE

Let us look closely at the tasks involved in your Historical Investigation.

Planning the Investigation (1)

Tasks:	Support and Guidance
Choose a broad *topic* within which you wish to set your investigation	Discuss with your teacher
Decide what the *purpose* of your Investigation will be	Discuss with your teacher
Decide the particular *issue(s)* you wish to investigate	

Points to note

- Your school will help you by offering resources for particular investigation topics. Make sure however that the issue(s) you choose to investigate are of real interest to you.

- It might be that you can choose issue(s) connected with what you have already studied in Standard Grade History. This could be very helpful.

- The issue(s) you decide upon must take the form of a question which you can examine or a statement which you can investigate. You cannot for instance look at 'Scotland during the First World War' because there is neither a question to examine nor a statement to investigate here. You could, however, examine a question such as 'How did the First World War affect the lives of people in Scotland?' or investigate a proposition or proposal such as 'The First World War changed the lives of Scottish people in many ways'.

Planning the Investigation (2)

Tasks:
Think of what is involved in investigating your issue(s).
Make a list of important *questions* that need to be looked at.

Points to note

- Keep a careful note of your decisions — the topic you have chosen, the issue(s) you wish to investigate, the important questions you must look at.

Planning the Investigation (3)

Tasks:	Support and Guidance
Begin to look for *historical evidence* to help you investigate the issue(s) by answering the questions you wish to look at.	See your teacher. As noted earlier, there might be useful resources in school.
	See pages 1–5 of this book to refresh your memory on types and variety of historical sources.
Think of other resources which might be of use in your Investigation.	School and public libraries, museums, heritage parks, public records offices, etc.

Points to note

- Do not hesitate to discuss your ideas with your class teacher.
- Try to be imaginative in thinking about possible sources. The more sources you use the more interesting your investigation will be.
- Keep a careful note of the sources you have used — what the source is, where you found it and so on.

Conducting the Investigation

Tasks:	Support and Guidance
Select those *sources* which provide useful evidence to help you answer the questions you wish to look at. *Extract* information from the evidence in the sources. *Note* and *record* this information.	For guidance on using evidence and working with historical sources see pages 5–14 of this book.

Points to note

- Make sure you know how to make best use of library resources (eg how to use catalogue and index-file systems to find items). Ask the librarian for help.
- Make sure you understand how to make best use of book and other printed items (eg how to use a book index or contents guide; how to 'skim-read' a section of a book). Your teacher will help here.
- How is your note-taking? As you work, try to improve your skills in making summaries, listing information, using headings, making use of tables and charts, drawing attention to 'key points' and so on.
- If you make use of oral (spoken) evidence (say by interviewing people, or using radio/TV or pre-recorded tape/cassettes) always make out a written transcript giving a full or summarised (condensed) written record of what is on tape.
- If you find useful evidence on film, video or computer data base ask your teacher to help you get the equipment you will need to study this.
- As always, keep a careful note of sources used, where you found the source, information contained in the source and so on.
- Keep a record or daily/weekly log (in diary form) of what you have done to date: books read, sources used, interviews, libraries and museums visited, etc. This will give you a useful check on where you are in your investigation exercise, and will be of great help in discussing progress with your class-teacher.

Presenting the Investigation

Tasks:	Support and Guidance
Present the outcome of your Investigation in an appropriate form of *Report*.	The Report can be written or can be in some other form. It might, for example, include tape, video or photographic materials.

Points to note

- Make sure your Report is clear and legible (readable).
- If you are including, for instance, tape/cassettes, photographs or maps, videotape, put these together in a suitable folder or pack them with the Report.

- Make sure that your Report — in whatever form you choose — is laid out in a sensible, orderly way, with an introduction giving the topic chosen and naming the issue(s) investigated, a main section dealing with the questions you examined, and a short final section stating the main findings of your Investigation.

- If your Report includes additional items like, for instance, photocopied sheets, reference pages, transcripts, bibliography (list of published materials you have read or used), put these in a separate section (normally at the end of your Report).

- If the Report is in written form, take great care over its final presentation. First, put together a rough 'draft' version of the Report. Second, spend some time carefully going over this, correcting, re-ordering sections if required, and trying to make sure that the whole Report fits together sensibly. Third, when you are happy with it, re-write or type up your final Report.

Leave plenty of time for this part of the exercise — it will take longer than you think!

THE HISTORICAL INVESTIGATION: KEYS TO SUCCESS

Planning your Investigation

- Is the issue likely to give rise to discussion: i.e. is there an issue to be investigated and will this involve making judgments?

- If the issue is likely to give rise only to describing without making judgments and drawing conclusions, **think again about your issue**.

- Have you broken down the issue into sub-headings or questions?

Conducting the Investigation; Selecting and Recording Information

- Use the sub-headings and questions in your plan as the working guide when looking for information. Try to provide sub-conclusions about the questions as you go through the report (see * below).

- When using information in your report, always state where you found the information and give as much detail on this as you can (e.g. title of book/article; page; author's name, etc.)

- In addition to giving details on particular information used in your report, provide a list of all resources you used (usually this would come at the end of your report).

Presenting the Findings of your Investigation

- Your report should follow the sub-headings and/or questions you set out in the plan of your investigation.

- The report must clearly refer all the way through to the issue you have chosen.

- There should be a clearly stated **conclusion** which relates to the issue.

- The conclusion should be clearly supported by the findings of your report. It might be a good idea, for instance, to provide * 'sub-conclusions' throughout your report so that the main conclusion is well supported.

CHAPTER · THREE ·
PRACTICE SECTION

The more you practise, the more you improve. The purpose of this section is to help you practise and improve the skills of historical study.

To help you get the maximum benefit from working through the Practice Section, the exercises have been set out as follows:

Practice exercises are grouped under the three main Course Units. All possible Contexts in the Standard Grade course are covered. Additional exercises are provided for the more popular Contexts. Some fully worked specimen answers are provided in the Appendix at the end of the book; these have guidance notes to help you improve your own answering techniques.

The form of each exercise is similar to that of the General and Credit examinations. This means you are learning exam techniques as you practise your historical study skills.

In each exercise there are three KU and three EV questions. The KU questions are similar to General KU exam items. At the end of the larger Contexts in all three course Units a selection of KU Credit questions, including extended writing items as found in the Credit examination, is provided.

EV questions provide a mix of General and Credit-type items.

Particular care has been taken to give you full coverage of all of the different types of KU and EV questions included in the Standard Grade examination.

*Note that **the order of questions shown (in the next column) is precisely the order of questions on every exercise page**. This will help you build up the precise skills needed in the Standard Grade Examination*

KU QUESTIONS

- Q1 DESCRIPTION: This type of question asks you to give an account of an event, development, or attitude shown by people in the past.

- Q2 EXPLANATION: This type of question asks you to give an explanation of causes and/or consequences or results of an event, development, action or attitude shown by people in the past.

- Q3 JUDGMENT: This type of question asks you to give a view or balanced explanation of an event, development, action or attitude shown by people in the past.

EV QUESTIONS

- Q1 EVALUATE EVIDENCE: This type of question asks you to assess the usefulness or reliability of a particular piece of historical source evidence. To do this you might look at various things like accuracy of the evidence, who wrote or created the source, whether the source is biased, or inconsistent and so on.

- Q2 COMPARE OR EXPLAIN POINTS OF VIEW as put forward or represented in different sources of evidence.

- Q3 PUT THE EVIDENCE INTO ITS HISTORICAL CONTEXT: This kind of task requires you to discuss the purpose, or the timing, or the particular significance of the evidence provided in the source or sources being looked at. You need to use your knowledge of actual historical background in answering this type of question.

UNIT 1 · CONTEXT A
Changing Scotland/Britain, 1750s–1850s
TECHNOLOGY/EMPLOYMENT — AGRICULTURE

▶ **SOURCE A** *Old Statistical Account, Parish of Carnwath, 1794:*

Turnip farming has lately been introduced, and bids fair to increase the rent of the lands and to better the conditions of the tenants. A few years ago there was no such thing known as a turnip-fed bullock or cow, but now there is not a tenant who does not feed 5 or 10, and some upwards of 20 black cattle every year ... each yielding from £2 to £3 profit ... After the turnip crop is sown barley, clover and rye grass.

▶ **SOURCE B** *Adapted from a secondary text:*

The Improvers increased greatly the value of land, so greater rents were demanded. In Perthshire, land was rented in 1750 at 5 shillings an acre; in 1795 it was 45 shillings.... For the wealthy farmer it was worthwhile paying the higher rents. The new farming produced heavier crops of better quality. The new turnpike roads allowed more markets to be reached. For the landlords the new rents produced such prosperity as they had never known before.

Not everyone prospered through the agricultural improvements.

▶ **SOURCE C** *Adapted from accounts written in the 1790s:*

Four or five of the small farms had been thrown into one farm. The whole was let to one of their number. My parents felt inclined to linger in the village and, as their house was let singly, they took it still for the coming year and became simply cottars, retaining nothing of their former stock but three or four barn-door hens.

The present (farm) occupant has managed to dispossess 7 or 8 dependent cottagers, who, from father to son had maintained themselves comfortably, brought up their children with decency and gave them a useful education. These, being turned adrift, found no other resources at least for their children than that of sending them to the factories.

▶ **SOURCE D** *Letter printed in the* Aberdeen Journal, *1774:*

There is not a better tract of cultivable land in Scotland than that we propose to leave. It is a grief to our spirits to leave it and our native land, and venture upon such a dangerous journey; but there is no help for it; we are not able to stand the high rents, and must do something for our bread or see our families reduced to beggary.

SECTION A: KU — GENERAL

1 Describe the 'new' farming introduced in the later eighteenth century in Scotland. (5)

2 For what reasons were farmers and landlords keen to change farming? Explain. (3)

3 What was the importance of the agricultural changes described for Scotland and Britain as a whole? (4)

SECTION B: EV — GEN/CREDIT

1 Do the authors of Sources C and D support the changes described? Explain. (4)

2 Compare the views on the effects of farming changes put forward in Sources A and C. (4)

3 Do the sources provide a full and accurate account of the effects of agricultural change in the eighteenth/early nineteenth centuries? Explain. (4)

UNIT 1 · CONTEXT A ·
Changing Scotland/Britain, 1750s–1850s
TECHNOLOGY/EMPLOYMENT — TEXTILE INDUSTRY

The domestic system was the older form of cloth-making in Britain.

▶ **SOURCE A** *From a secondary text:*

Work was done in the home. Most cottagers could make or afford to buy the simple tools needed. The weaver's cottage was his workshop. His children washed the wool and removed bits and pieces clinging to the fleece. His wife and daughters spun the wool into yarn on a spinning wheel or on the older distaff and spindle. The weaver wove the yarn into cloth on a hand loom. He also probably owned a few acres of land and grew enough to keep his family.

▶ **SOURCE B** *Adapted from The Old Statistical Account, Parish of Hamilton, 1791:*

The state of manufactures has of late undergone considerable change. They get employment from the great manufacturers in Glasgow and cotton yarn is the principal material. Young women, formerly put to the spinning wheel now learn to flower muslin and apply to the same Glasgow manufacturers for employment.

▶ **SOURCE C** *Cotton mill, 1835.*

Often we may see, in a single building a 100 horse-power steam-engine which has the strength of 880 men, set in motion 50,000 spindles. The whole requires the service of but 750 workers, but these machines, with the assistance of that mighty power, can produce as much yarn as formerly could have been spun by 200,000 men ... The 50,000 spindles together will produce in 12 hours a thread 62,000 English miles in length that would encircle the whole Earth two and a half times ...

▶ **SOURCE D** *Spinning by steam.*

▶ **SOURCE E** *From the* Leeds Mercury, *1830:*

Thousands of children, male and female, are compelled by the appalling thong or strap of the overseer to rush, half-dressed but not half-fed, to infantile slavery in the mills in the town of Bradford. Thousands of little children, principally female, from 7 to 14 years of age are forced to labour from 6 o'clock in the morning to 7 o'clock in the evening, with only — Britons blush while you read it! — with only 30 minutes allowed for eating and recreation.

SECTION A: KU — GENERAL

1. What changes in textile manufacture took place in eighteenth century Scotland? (5)

2. What effect did these changes have on the people who worked in the industry? (4)

3. How important were changes in the textile industry for other industries in eighteenth/nineteenth century Britain? (3)

SECTION B: EV — GEN/CREDIT

1. Is the writer of Source C in favour of the changes he describes? Explain your answer. (3)

2. Do Sources D and E give differing views of work in textile mills in the 1830s? Explain. (4)

3. Do you believe the evidence about work in the textile mills provided in Source E? Explain your answer. (5)

UNIT 1 · CONTEXT A ·
Changing Scotland/Britain, 1750s–1850s
POPULATION GROWTH AND DISTRIBUTION

▶ **SOURCE A** *From* A Tour in Scotland and Voyage to Hebrides *(1772):*

The people are most wretched: their most miserable hovels, made of poles wattled and covered with thin sods. There is not sufficient corn raised to supply half the wants of the inhabitants. Numbers were migrating; they wandered in a state of desperation; too poor to pay, they sell themselves for passage, preferring a temporary bondage in a strange land to starving in their native soil.

▶ **SOURCE B** *Estate factor's evidence to Board of Agriculture (1811):*

Sheep farms are paying well on the Sutherland estates. The numbers of Cheviot sheep are now about 15,000. More ground will be laid out for the same husbandry without decreasing the population. Situations will be fixed on for the people: fishing stations, inland villages with textile machinery. The industrious will be protected but the lazy must leave or starve.

▶ **SOURCE C** *Selected population statistics.*

Glasgow	25,000 (1750)	200,000 (1831)
Paisley	17,000 (1782)	31,000 (1801)
Monklands	8,700 (1801)	45,000 (1841)

Number emigrating from:

	Scotland	Ireland	England & Wales
1815–34	30,000	420,000	100,000
1835–50	80,000	1,409,000	320,000
1851–60	183,000	1,231,000	640,000

▶ **SOURCE D** *Sketch — Irish house (1840s).*

SECTION A: KU — GENERAL

1 What were the main features of population change in Scotland in the late seventeenth and early eighteenth centuries? (4)

2 What were the causes of population migration in Scotland 1750–1850? (4)

3 Did Scots suffer more hardship than others in Britain in the period 1750–1850? Explain. (4)

SECTION B: EV — GEN/CREDIT

1 Compare the value of Sources A and B as evidence of life in the Scottish Highlands in the periods indicated. (5)

2 Do Sources A and D give similar or differing accounts of the poor in Scotland and Ireland? (3)

3 Do the sources accurately cover all aspects of population change? Explain. (4)

UNIT 1 · CONTEXT A ·
Changing Scotland/Britain, 1750s–1850s
REFORM — RADICAL UNREST

▶ **SOURCE A** *Radical William Cobbett, writing in 1816:*

The cause of our present miseries, is the enormous amount of taxes the government makes us pay to support its army, policemen, pensioners etc. The remedy is a reform in the House of Commons or People's House of Parliament to allow members to be selected annually.

At St Peter's Field, Manchester, in August 1819, a radical protest meeting was held.

▶ **SOURCE B** *From a radical publication of the time:*

Before 12 o'clock crowds began to assemble, each town or hamlet having a banner, and some a cap with 'Liberty' upon it: each party, as they came through the streets, kept a military order, with sticks shouldered. A banner was printed 'Taxation and no representation is ... unjust' and on the reverse '... Equal representation or death'. On another banner 'Die like men, and not be sold like slaves'. On a third 'Major Cartwright's Bill and no Corn Laws', on a fourth '... Strength and Liberty'. It was 20 minutes after 1 o'clock before Hunt (the main speaker at the meeting) appeared. 'Gentlemen, I must entreat that you will be peaceable: a great deal depends on that.'

▶ **SOURCE C** *Eye-witness account:*

About half-past one, the magistrates read the Riot Act, and instantly the platform was surrounded in a masterly manner ... The mob assaulted the military and civil authorities with ... missiles. Consequently the cavalry charged in their own defence; not without first being witnesses to a pistol-shot from the crowd.

▶ **SOURCE D** *Another eye-witness account:*

An undisciplined body led on by officers who had never had any experience in military affairs and probably under the influence both of personal fear and considerable political feeling of hostility, could not be expected to act either with coolness or discrimination ... men, women and children ... were equally exposed to their attack. Numbers were trampled and cut down.

▶ **SOURCE E**

SECTION A: KU — GENERAL

1 What were the main demands of the Radicals in early nineteenth century Britain? (4)

2 Why did Mr Hunt ask the audience to be 'peaceable' at the meeting? (3)

3 How important was the Radical Movement in the development of political democracy in Britain in the early nineteenth century? Fully explain. (5)

SECTION B: EV — GEN/CREDIT

1 How useful are Sources B, C, D and E as evidence of what happened at St Peter's Field? (5)

2 Do Sources C and D provide consistently similar accounts of events at the meeting? (3)

3 Do the sources give an accurate and justifiable representation of the views of the authorities towards political change? Explain. (4)

· UNIT 1 · CONTEXT A ·
Changing Scotland/Britain, 1750s–1850s
SOCIAL CONDITIONS: HEALTH AND HOUSING

▶ **SOURCE A** *Glasgow, 1819:*

If any man wonders at the fever among the lower classes, take the walk which I did today, along an alley four feet wide, flanked by houses five floors high, with here and there a pool of water, from which there is no drain, and in which all the waste of the neighbourhood is deposited, to putrefy and rot.

▶ **SOURCE B** *Sheffield, about 1820:*

Perhaps the most hideous town in Creation... All ups and downs and back-slums. Volumes of black smoke veil the sun and the blue sky even on the brightest day. More than one crystal stream runs sparkling down the valleys and enters the town but they soon get defiled and creep through the town heavily charged with dyes, clogged with rotting waste and bubbling with poisonous gases.

▶ **SOURCE C** *A cartoon of the 1850s.*

A Court For King Cholera

▶ **SOURCE D** *Adapted from a secondary text:*

The 1848 Public Health Act established local Boards of Health... to have general powers of cleansing, sewerage and drainage, and to ensure a 'proper and sufficient' water supply. The General Board of Health of London had its own doctors and engineers to advise local authorities... By 1854 local Boards had been set up in nearly 200 towns.

▶ **SOURCE E** *Comment (written in 1849):*

In our district so extensive,
If a drain's at all offensive,
It must instantly be mended,
Which is monstrously expensive.
And the dead we're forced to bury
Somewhere in a cemetery, all because our
 churchyard's crowded...
We, the Board of Health supposes,
Ought to make sinks smell like roses.
People nowadays pretend to have such very
 dainty noses...

SECTION A: KU — GENERAL

1 In what ways were housing and public health conditions inadequate in towns such as Glasgow and Sheffield? (4)

2 Why did poor housing and lack of concern for public health contribute to disease? (4)

3 Why were diseases such as cholera so important in nineteenth century Britain? Explain. (4)

SECTION B: EV — GEN/CREDIT

1 Do Sources C and E give exaggerated or biased views? Explain your answer. (4)

2 Do Sources A, B and C give consistent views of nineteenth century urban conditions? Explain. (4)

3 How typical were the views expressed in Source E among British people in the 1840s? Explain. (4)

UNIT 1 · CONTEXT A ·
Changing Scotland/Britain, 1750s–1850s
PARLIAMENTARY REFORM — BEFORE AND AFTER 1832

▶ **SOURCE A** *Parliamentary elections before 1832 (contemporary accounts).*

(1) When the county of Caithness returns a Member, he is nominated by Sir John Sinclair. The County of Cromarty is under the influence of Henry Davidson, Esq., and the County of Kinross, of Thomas Graham, Esq. The late Lord Melville always boasted that he could return thirty-nine out of the forty-five who represented the whole kingdom of Scotland!

(2) Glasgow's number of inhabitants exceeds 77,000; its delegate is chosen by thirty-two members of the town council, who are all self-elected; and this delegate has only one voice of four in the choice of a Member of Parliament with the delegates of three little towns.

▶ **SOURCE B** *Adapted from 'Electing an MP' (fictional account):*

Thomas Bowet (a newly elected town councillor), not being versed in election matters consulted ... the Dean of Guild as to the way of voting ... 'Ye'll just say as I'll say, and I'll say what Bailie Shaw says, for he will do what my lord bids him', which was as peaceful a way of sending up a Member of Parliament as could well be devised.

In 1832 the Whigs introduced the First Reform Act.

▶ **SOURCE C** *From a secondary text:*

The bill ... passed in June 1832 was a very moderate reform which enfranchised (gave the vote to) none of the working men who had paraded so enthusiastically, but rather strengthened the position of the middle classes. In Scotland the seats were increased and redistributed so that twenty-three were allocated to the burghs, including some of the new industrial towns, all householders who paid a rent of at least ten pounds (a fairly high figure in those days) being entitled to vote... The number of MPs for the counties remained thirty as before ... The vote was given to all freeholders of land worth ten pounds a year and tenants of land worth fifty pounds ... Although the Reform Act was limited in its scope, it marked a break with the old system and paved the way for other reforms.

▶ **SOURCE D** *Political cartoon. Popular electioneering, 1841.*

SECTION A: KU — GENERAL

1. In what ways were elections before 1832 unrepresentative and unfair? (3)

2. Who was mainly responsible for the unrepresentativeness of parliamentary elections before 1832? Explain fully. (4)

3. How important was the 1832 Reform Act in the development of democracy in Britain? (5)

SECTION B: EV — GEN/CREDIT

1. How useful is Source A as evidence of how MPs were elected before 1832? (4)

2. In what ways do Sources A and B support the view that elections before 1832 were unfair? (4)

3. Do Sources C and D give a reliable and accurate view of the effects of the 1832 Act? Explain your answer fully. (4)

UNIT 1 · CONTEXT A
Changing Scotland/Britain, 1750s–1850s
CREDIT LEVEL — KU QUESTIONS

1 *While the population of Britain as a whole increased notably during the eighteenth and nineteenth centuries, what was more notable was how the distribution of population also changed.*

Describe the main changes in population distribution in Britain between 1750 and 1850. (4)

2 *From the mid eighteenth century onwards, Britain was increasingly transformed by what came to be called the First Industrial Revolution.*

Taking the example of the textile industry, discuss the main results of technological change during the late eighteenth and nineteenth centuries in Britain. (4)

3 *As industrialisation progressed, the living conditions of the ever-growing industrial workforce deteriorated. The state of public health became an unavoidable concern by the 1830s.*

What was the importance of poor housing as a cause of deteriorating health among the industrial working classes during this period? (4)

4 *The factory rather than the farm or cottage became the centre of manufacturing. Neither on land nor in the factories did working conditions improve.*

Choosing *either* work on the land *or* work in the textile industry, discuss changing working conditions during the period 1750 to 1850.
For this answer you should write a short essay of several paragraphs. (8)

5 *The 1832 Reform Act was more important as a signal for future change rather than an instant transformation in parliamentary reform.*

Explain the importance of the First Reform Act in the development of parliamentary reform in Britain. (4)

UNIT 1 · CONTEXT B
Changing Scotland/Britain, 1830s–1930s
TECHNOLOGY/EMPLOYMENT: ON THE LAND

▶ **SOURCE A** *Steam-powered threshing, 1850s.*

▶ **SOURCE B** *Adapted from an account of Victorian farming, 1850:*

One day we learned the processes ... for economising labour, manure and food; and the next day we saw ... manure created as a troublesome nuisance; and cattle kept starving in the open fields in winter. The same day we saw the steam engine by which the farmer is enabled to thrash his wheat crop for one penny a bushel we found other farmers paying four or five times as much for the same operation, not so well done by hand.

▶ **SOURCE C** *1840s–mid 1870s.*

The golden age of British agriculture lasted until the mid 1870s. British farming became the most advanced in Europe ... and as long as the farmer had the advantage of being close to his market, he could meet the growing demand for wheat, mutton and beef without fear of foreign competition. Railways carried his produce to the towns rapidly and cheaply, and brought him supplies of cattle feed, fertiliser and machinery ... Railways stimulated most industries and farmers benefited from the general rise in prosperity as people spent more on buying food.

▶ **SOURCE D** *Late 1870s–1890s.*

The original cause of the farmer's misfortune was the invasion of grain from North America. This was due chiefly to steam shipping and the expansion of railways in the USA ... Distance now afforded the English farmer no protection ... No sooner had many farmers begun to switch over to pastoral farming than foreign competition was felt as a result of the development of refrigerated sea transport ... Imports of mutton rose, while beef arrived in increasing quantities from Argentina and North America.

SECTION A: KU — GENERAL

1 In what ways did technology assist British farming between the 1830s and 1870s? (4)

2 Explain why technology created problems as well as opportunities for British farming. (3)

3 How important was the widening of markets in the development of British farming between the 1850s and 1870s? Explain fully. (5)

SECTION B: EV — GEN/CREDIT

1 Did the author of Source B support reform in farming? Give reasons for your answer. (3)

2 Do Sources A and B together give a balanced account of farming in the 1850s? Explain. (4)

3 Is the view of farming progress given in Source B one which was shared by everyone involved in British farming? Explain your answer fully. (5)

UNIT 1 · CONTEXT B ·
Changing Scotland/Britain, 1830s–1930s
TECHNOLOGY: RAILWAYS

▶ **SOURCE A** *Cartoon comment on the coming of the railway.*

▶ **SOURCE B** *From a secondary text:*

The railway brought manufacturers within range of new raw materials, cut their costs, and opened up vast markets to their goods. Perishable goods could now be sold far afield, bringing a new prosperity to farmers and fishermen, and workers could travel the country in search of jobs. Railway building meant a huge demand for coal and iron. And since speeds of 50–60 mph were already possible by 1850 the circulation of newspapers and letters was already being transformed.

▶ **SOURCE C** *Adapted from the New Statistical Account of Scotland:*

Four great railways pass through this parish ... beside these the Monkland and Glasgow Canal extends through almost the entire length of the parish. The revenue of the canal may be £15,000 per annum, and that of the railways £20,000 ... The Garnkirk Railway Company run a train of carriages by steam four times a day between Glasgow and Airdrie; open carriages 8d, closed carriages 1s. The canal boat runs twice a day; fares 4d steerage, 6d cabin. The steam trains go in an hour, the canal boats in two hours. ... The canal rates have been reduced since the introduction of railways nearly one third, and yet the railway is in a thriving condition.

▶ **SOURCE D** *Some legislation.*

1801–25	Acts setting up many local railway companies in England.
1838–41	Acts setting up long-distance railways e.g. Manchester–London.
1840–42	Acts regulating safety, building standards, rates and fares.
1844	Cheap Trains Act — 1d per mile 'working class trains'.
1846	Gauge Act — laying down standard width of rail track.
1846–1900	Frequent Acts on safety regulations, hours of work.

SECTION A: KU — GENERAL

1. What were the main results of the coming of railways in Britain in the 1830–1850 period? (4)

2. Who benefited from the development of railways in Britain, and why did they do so? (4)

3. Why were there increasing numbers of laws relating to railways in Britain as the nineteenth century progressed? (4)

SECTION B: EV — GEN/CREDIT

1. How useful is Source C as evidence of transport developments in Scotland in the 1840s? (4)

2. In what ways do Sources A and C give different viewpoints on the importance of railways? (3)

3. Does Source A or Source C provide the more reliable and accurate evidence about transport in nineteenth century Britain? Fully explain. (5)

· UNIT 1 · CONTEXT B ·
Changing Scotland/Britain, 1830s–1930s
HOUSING AND HEALTH

▶ **SOURCE A** *Royal Commission, 1844:*

The poorer classes are exposed to causes of disease and death. The result is the same as if 20,000 ... were annually taken out of these wretched dwellings and put to death, the actual fact being that they are allowed to remain in them to die.

▶ **SOURCE B**

1868 Local Councils given power to demolish insanitary/dangerous houses.

1875 Local Councils given power to clear slum houses and build council houses.

1884 Royal Commission reported urban overcrowding and lack of sanitation as bad as that described forty years before by the 1844 Royal Commission.

1890 Housing Act compelling Local Councils to demolish the worst slums.

▶ **SOURCE C** *A city slum, 1870s.*

▶ **SOURCE D** *Housing in the 1930s.*

Although an industrial town, Wishaw was surrounded by beautiful estates. The Town Council acquired a part of one of these estates and this ... became the setting for an avenue of houses, built in pairs or in fours, all with gardens at the front and at the back. The houses varied in size from living-room and two bedrooms with bathroom and kitchen to living-room, dining-room and three bedrooms also with bathroom and kitchen ... The old slum houses were torn down and new houses erected on the sites. Sometimes the sites were transformed into public parks and playing fields with special enclosures for younger children with swings, see-saws and sandpits.

▶ **SOURCE E** *Saint Salandar's Close, Dundee, 1920s.*

SECTION A: KU — GENERAL

1 What were the commonest causes of disease and death in nineteenth century urban Britain? (3)

2 Why were the causes of disease and death not effectively dealt with until the twentieth century? (5)

3 Why did parliament put such importance upon giving greater powers to local councils during the nineteenth century? (4)

SECTION B: EV — GEN/CREDIT

1 How useful are Sources A and C as evidence on housing between 1840 and 1880? (4)

2 Do Sources B and C provide similar or differing impressions of city life in the times indicated? (3)

3 Does Source D or Source E give the more typical and accurate description of housing in Scotland in the 1920s and 1930s? Explain fully. (5)

UNIT 1 · CONTEXT B ·
Changing Scotland/Britain, 1830s–1930s
EMPLOYMENT/WORK CONDITIONS: COAL MINING

▶ **SOURCE A** *From the Report of the Royal Commission on Mines, 1842:*

In some cases children are taken into mines to work as early as four years of age ... from eight to nine is the ordinary age at which employment in these mines commences ... From six years old and upwards, the hard work of pushing and dragging the carriages of coal begins. When the work people are in full employment, the regular hours of work for children and young persons are rarely less than eleven, in some districts thirteen or fourteen. Accidents of a fearful nature are very frequent.

▶ **SOURCE B** *Poem on miners:*

... From the depth where night presides,
With winking taper, o'er the inback'd slave,
Who, laid face upward, hews the black stone
　　down.
Poor living corpse; he labours in the grave,
Poor two-legged mole; he mines for
　　half-a-crown,
From morn to eve ...

▶ **SOURCE C** *At the coal-face.*

▶ **SOURCE D** *Coalmining legislation.*

1842　Mines Act: No employment of women and children underground. No child under ten to be employed.

1850　Mines Act: Government Inspectors appointed. Safety rules applied.

1855　Mines Safety Act: Further safety rules passed as 'General Rules'.

1860　Regulations Act: No children under twelve who were below an agreed standard of education to be employed.

1872　Coal Mines Act: Mine managers to possess certificate of technical knowledge. Daily inspection of pits for safety.

▶ **SOURCE E**

> In Remembrance of the
> **UNFORTUNATE SUFFERERS,**
> WHO
> **LOST THEIR LIVES**
> IN THE OAKS COLLIERY EXPLOSION,
> BARNSLEY,
> DECEMBER 12, 1866,
> WHEN UPWARDS OF
> 350 Souls were Launched into Eternity.
>
> The Angel of Death spread his wings on the blast,
> And the eyes of the sleepers wax'd deadly and chill,
> In the face of the miner he breathed as he pass'd ;
> And their hearts but once heav'd, and for ever grew still.
> "Prepare to meet thy God."

SECTION A: KU — GENERAL

1 What were the main problems for children working underground in British coalmines? (4)

2 Why did working conditions fail to improve very much during the nineteenth century? (4)

3 How important was parliamentary legislation in bettering conditions in British mines? (4)

SECTION B: EV — GEN/CREDIT

1 How useful is Source A as evidence on working conditions in British mines in the 1840s? (4)

2 Compare the ways in which Sources A, B, C and E offer similar or differing evidence on mining. (5)

3 Do you think the description of a coalminer's life given in Source B is accurate? Explain. (3)

UNIT 1 · CONTEXT B ·
Changing Scotland/Britain, 1830s–1930s
EXTENSION OF THE FRANCHISE 1867–1884

▶ **SOURCE A** *From a secondary text:*

The 1867 Bill almost doubled the number qualified to vote to just under two millions. Though 50 burghs still had fewer than 500 and although 500,000 people in small country towns returned more MPs than the ten million of London, the Midlands and the industrial North, the Act was a turning point in politics. For the first time a majority of the electorate were town dwellers. This forced politicians to face problems before ignored. Many expected that both parties would bid for the support of the working man.

▶ **SOURCE B** *Liberal leader Gladstone campaigning (1876).*

▶ **SOURCE C** *Liberal Party policies.*

The essential feature of the Liberal Federation is the principle of the direct participation of all members of the party in the direction of party affairs.

▶ **SOURCE D** *Conservative policies.*

The Conservative party will never exercise power until it has the confidence of the working classes. If you want to gain this, let them have a large share — a real share — in party councils and party government.

▶ **SOURCE E** *From a secondary text:*

In 1884 the right to vote was given to voters in county elections on the same terms as in the burghs, the two million new voters included farm labourers, and such industrial workers as miners who lived outside the main towns. A further measure in 1885 divided the country into roughly equal constituencies, so ending the over-representation of the southern farming counties.

SECTION A: KU — GENERAL

1 Describe changes in electoral rules in Britain between 1867 and 1884. (4)

2 Why did electoral reform continue after 1867? (3)

3 How important were the reforms of the 1860s to 1880s for British democracy? (5)

SECTION B: EV — GEN/CREDIT

1 How useful are Sources B and C as evidence of the effects of electoral reform on British political life? (4)

2 Do Sources B, C and D give similar views on politics in the 1870s? Explain your answer. (4)

3 How justifiable were the views put forward in Sources C and D? Explain. (4)

UNIT 1 · CONTEXT B ·
Changing Scotland/Britain, 1830s–1930s
PARLIAMENTARY REFORM — WOMEN'S SUFFRAGE

The Suffragette campaign became more violent after 1903.

▶ **SOURCE A** *From a secondary text:*

The women's Social and Political Union (WSPU) was set up in 1903 ... Mrs Pankhurst's followers believed that women would only get the vote if they protested. ... These 'suffragettes' heckled at public meetings, chained themselves to railings at Downing Street and Buckingham Palace, smashed shop windows ... — all to draw attention to their case ...

▶ **SOURCE B** *A Punch cartoon.*

Militant Suffragist (after long and futile efforts to light a fire for her tea-kettle): 'And to think that only yesterday I burnt two pavilions and a church!'

▶ **SOURCE C** *Mrs Pankhurst, 1912:*

The argument of the broken window-pane is the most valuable argument in modern politics.

▶ **SOURCE D** *From a secondary text:*

Lloyd George sent for Mrs Pankhurst and asked if she would organise a great recruiting campaign amongst women for work in munition factories ... Mrs Pankhurst responded gladly. ... Soon women were working at all manner of employments in which, a year or two earlier their presence would have been deplored. They eased the labour problem and it was a foregone conclusion that the vote was as good as theirs. It became legal with the Fourth Franchise Bill of 1918, in which the vote was given to all women over thirty.

▶ **SOURCE E** *Lord Birkenhead (memoirs):*

It was in the year 1918, after the War, that the disaster took place ... Let me describe how, inevitably, we descended the slipping slope. First of all it was not proposed that women should be included (in the extension of voting rights). Then a member of the House of Commons said that whoever was ... not included, it was quite impossible to exclude ... the brave men who had supported our cause in the field. ... That argument was accepted ... Then another member of the House arose and said: 'If you are extending the franchise to our brave soldiers ... how about our brave munition workers?' That argument too ... was difficult to resist ... Then a subtle member of the House said: 'How about our brave women munition workers?'. And, having yielded to the first argument it was absolutely impossible to resist the second.

SECTION A: KU — GENERAL

1 Describe the methods used by Suffragettes in their campaigns. (4)

2 Why did some Suffragettes believe it necessary to use violence? (4)

3 Was the First World War the most important turning point in the winning of votes for women? Explain. (4)

SECTION B: EV — GEN/CREDIT

1 How useful are Sources B and E in showing the attitudes of the cartoonist and writer involved? (3)

2 Do Sources D and E agree or disagree on the reasons for women gaining the vote? Explain. (4)

3 How accurately do the sources represent the attitudes of the people of Britain towards the idea of votes for women? Fully explain. (5)

· UNIT 1 · CONTEXT B ·
Changing Scotland/Britain, 1830s–1930s
POPULATION: MIGRATION

There was steady movement of people from the Highlands after the 1740s.

▶ **SOURCE A**   Chamber's Journal, *1837:*

We are told that there are a hundred thousand people . . . starving in wretched mud hovels on the barren sea-shores of the Highlands and Islands. We would ask persons in power to form some system for the gradual removal . . . of the Highlanders to the great seats of industry.

▶ **SOURCE B**   *Adapted from* Illustrated London News, *1853:*

His Royal Highness Prince Albert has become Patron of the Highland & Island Emigration Society . . . Since the end of May 1852 it has sent to Australia 3000 people. HMS Hercules is now in the harbour of Campbeltown receiving immigrants to aid the relief of distress in these islands caused by excess of population and at the same time aid the relief of distress in Australia caused by short supply of labourers.

▶ **SOURCE C**   *From 'The Canadian Boat Song':*

From the lone shieling of the misty island
Mountains divide us and the waste of sea
Yet still the blood is strong, the heart
   is Highland
And we in dreams behold the Hebrides
When the bold kindred in the time long
   vanished
Conquered the soil and fortified the keep
No seer foretold the children would be
   banished
That a degenerate lord might boast his sheep.

Another kind of immigrant was arriving in Lowland Scotland at this time.

▶ **SOURCE D**   *From a secondary text:*

By 1841 there were at least 125,000 Irish-born persons in Scotland, most of them in Clydeside . . . The 'Potato Famine' almost doubled their number. The 'Irish Invasion' as it was called by a Glasgow newspaper of the time, caused much bitter feeling among Scottish people. In 1849, the authorities in Glasgow, already grossly overcrowded, began to send Irish paupers back to their own country at a rate of 1,000 a month . . . By 1851 about a quarter of Glasgow's 360,000 inhabitants were Irish . . . Jealousy of the Irishmen as incomers and as rival competitors for the jobs available combined with a revival of old anti-Catholic bitterness . . . to produce many scenes of violence, the 'Orange and Green riots' . . . Irish men and women still continued to come over mostly for permanent work in Clyde shipyards but some . . . in large bands of 'tattie-howkers' for the potato-harvest.

SECTION A: KU — GENERAL

1 Describe the main features of population movements in and out of Scotland during the 1830s and 1850s. (4)

2 Explain the causes of migration within and outside Scotland between 1830 and 1860. (4)

3 Was emigration or immigration more important in the historical development of Scotland in the nineteenth century? Explain your answer. (4)

SECTION B: EV — GEN/CREDIT

1 How useful are Sources A and B as evidence of Scottish migration in the 1830s and 1850s? (4)

2 In what ways do Sources A and B give similar views on the importance of migration? (4)

3 Why is Source C a significant piece of evidence in explaining attitudes of Scots people towards migration? Explain your answer. (4)

UNIT 1 · CONTEXT B ·
Changing Scotland/Britain, 1830s–1930s
HEALTH AND HOUSING — THE POOR

▶ **SOURCE A** *Workhouse rules, 1835:*

As soon as a pauper is admitted he shall be ... clothed in a workhouse dress ... The paupers shall be classed as follows ...

Class 1: Men infirm ... Class 2: Able-bodied men and youths above 15. Class 3: Boys above 7 and under 15. Class 4: Women infirm ... Class 5: Able-bodied women and girls above 15. Class 6: Girls above 7 and under 15. Class 7: Children under 7 years.

To each class shall be assigned a ward ... The master of the workhouse shall allow the father or mother of any child in the same workhouse ... to have an interview with such child one time in each day.

▶ **SOURCE B** *Anti-Poor Law writer, 1838:*

The Poor Law is cruel and illegal ... one of degradation and starvation for the poor. The real object is to punish poverty as a crime ... Children and parents are dying frequently in the same bastille without ... knowing of one another's fate.

▶ **SOURCE C** *A farm labourer's cottage in 1872.*

The source below describes working class poverty in London around 1900.

▶ **SOURCE D** *Social Report, London East End, 1903 (extracts):*

No 70 Alpha Street: A labourer, aged thirty, nine weeks out of employment; three children at school, one baby ... All have been ill with bad throats ... Second family: a labourer aged twenty-nine, five weeks out of employment; two children at school, two babies; selling things for food. Third family: A labourer aged twenty-seven, seventeen weeks out of employment; three babies; living in one room; receiving three shillings a week from parish; no coal, very desolate.

SECTION A: KU — GENERAL

1 Describe the ways in which the comfort and health of families was affected by life in a workhouse. (4)

2 What were the causes of poverty for workhouse and farm labourers' families as shown in Sources B and C? (4)

3 To what extent did those in authority appear to put the blame for poverty upon the poor themselves? Explain your answer. (4)

SECTION B: EV — GEN/CREDIT

1 How useful are Sources B and D as evidence of poor living conditions in 1838 and 1903? (4)

2 To what extent do the sources offer similar or different impressions of poverty in the nineteenth and twentieth centuries? Explain your answer. (4)

3 Does Source D accurately represent widespread living conditions among Britain's poor at the beginning of the twentieth century? Explain. (4)

UNIT 1 · CONTEXT B ·
Changing Scotland/Britain, 1830s–1930s
CREDIT LEVEL — KU QUESTIONS

1. *Economic change was the driving force behind the shifting population movements in industrialising Britain in the eighteenth and nineteenth centuries.*

   Describe the main features of population movement within Britain between 1830 and the 1930s. (4)

2. *The Industrial Revolution was firmly based upon technological improvement, and the existence of a workforce ready to adapt to rapid change.*

   Explain the effects of technological change in either coalmining or railway developments between the 1830s and 1900s.
   For this question you should write a short essay of several paragraphs. (8)

3. *'If a drain's at all offensive, it must instantly be mended. We, the Board of Health supposes, ought to make sinks smell like roses.'*

   How important was the issue of public health for people living in Britain in the latter half of the nineteenth century? Explain your answer. (4)

4. *'Poor living corpse, he labours in the grave, Poor two-legged mule, he mines for half-a-crown from morn till eve.'*

   Did working conditions in coalmining improve or deteriorate between the 1830s and the 1930s? Explain your answer. (4)

5. *'The working class are determined to govern themselves and will not be hoodwinked by any class or class interests.'*

   How important was the Second Reform Act of 1867 in bringing about political democracy in Britain? Explain your answer. (4)

· UNIT 1 · CONTEXT C ·
Changing Scotland/Britain, 1880s–present
TECHNOLOGICAL CHANGE — TRANSPORT

▶ **SOURCE A** *20 mph speed limit, 1903.*

A POLICE TRAP

'I say Bill, We can't be doing more than twenty miles an hour! What do you think?'

▶ **SOURCE B** *Adapted from a secondary text:*

Cars remained for some years as possessions only of the rich. Daimlers were made at Coventry and at the 1909 Motor Show the Rolls-Royce 'Silver Cloud' was exhibited.... As early as 1901 cars had assumed their modern shape, with the engine in front of the driver, but they were high and roofless. Motoring on country roads which had not been 'macadamised' caused clouds of dust, and both men and women took to motoring goggles and long enveloping coats.

▶ **SOURCE C** *Adapted from a secondary text:*

Before 1910 ... The Great North Road from London to Carlisle was under the control of 72 separate (local) authorities ... not one of which had powers to make a yard of new road to by-pass troublespots. No government department was responsible for roads.

▶ **SOURCE D** *Adapted from a speech by Lloyd George, 1909:*

Our present system of roads and road-making is inadequate ... The State has done nothing at all for our roads.

The growing motor age in Britain, 1930s to 1960s.

▶ **SOURCE E** *Facts and figures.*

Road vehicles (millions)

	1938	1958	1968
Cars	1.9	4.6	10.8
Lorries and vans	0.5	1.3	1.6
Public transport	0.1	0.1	0.1

▶ **SOURCE F** *Car assembly works, 1960s.*

SECTION A: KU — GENERAL

1 Give a short account of road transport developments in Britain between 1900 and 1910. (4)

2 What major road transport problems had been brought about by the 1960s in Britain? (3)

3 How important has the motor car been in the social and economic development of modern Britain? Fully explain your answer. (5)

SECTION B: EV — GEN/CREDIT

1 What examples of bias and exaggeration can be found in Source A? Explain your answer. (3)

2 Contrast the value of Sources A, D and F as evidence of transport changes in twentieth century Britain. (4)

3 Do the sources fully represent all aspects of road transport development in twentieth century Britain? Explain your answer. (5)

UNIT 1 · CONTEXT C ·
Changing Scotland/Britain, 1880s–present
TECHNOLOGICAL CHANGE — SHIPBUILDING

The two world wars directly affected twentieth century British shipbuilding.

▶ **SOURCE A** *Shipbuilding trends.*

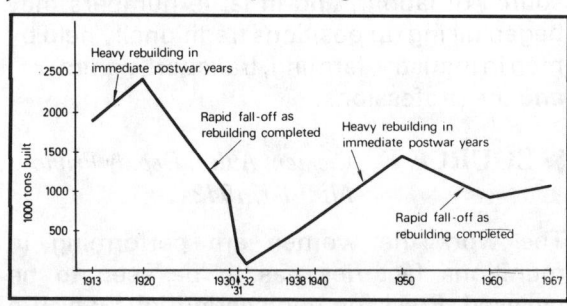

Ups and downs of shipbuilding in the twentieth century

▶ **SOURCE B** *Adapted from a memoir (1958):*

My own firm (Motherwell Bridge & Engineering Co) did important war work (1939–45) ... One of the greatest achievements was the laying down of a complete shipyard on the banks of the Forth at Alloa. Altogether two thousand people were employed there. Nearly a hundred transport landing craft were launched at the Alloa yard. We had a share too in the construction of a large number of frigates. The component structures were welded in large units and sent to the shipyards on the Clyde for assembly ... My firm ... with John Brown & Co Ltd, the famous shipbuilders, worked ... on the conversion of large liners to aircraft-carriers.

▶ **SOURCE C** *From a secondary text:*

The British Government gave less encouragement in the form of subsidies which most foreign governments gave their shipyards ... Relations between management and men in British yards were far from good ... The frequent disputes and stoppages of work often led to late deliveries and setbacks to Britain's reputation as a shipbuilder. An enquiry of 1966 concluded that there were too many shipyards in the country and that they were too small ... Four yards on the Tyne merged. Similar mergers took place on the Clyde: John Brown, Fairfield, Alexander Stephen and Connell came together as the Upper Clyde Shipbuilders.

▶ **SOURCE D** *From a secondary text:*

The Second World War revived the industry, and, when it was over, the destruction of shipyards in Germany and Japan gave Britain an excellent opportunity. She failed to take it. Our industry was out of date while the craft unions held endless strikes over who-does-what disputes. Between the wars we had still produced half the world's tonnage but by 1956 our share had fallen to 14 per cent. Germany was ... ahead of us and Japan even more so. She now builds twice as many ships as her three closest rivals. Our own industry stays alive only with the aid of massive grants from the government.

SECTION A: KU — GENERAL

1. In what ways did war affect the British shipbuilding industry in the twentieth century? (3)

2. For what reasons has British shipbuilding generally declined during the century? (5)

3. How important were government actions and attitudes in bringing about changes in British shipbuilding in the 1950s and 1960s? (4)

SECTION B: EV — GEN/CREDIT

1. How useful are Sources A and B in describing British shipbuilding during this century? (4)

2. What similarities and differences can you detect in the reasons for shipbuilding decline as presented in Sources C and D? (4)

3. Do you believe the causes of shipbuilding decline on the Clyde and Tyne as given in Source C? Explain your answer. (4)

UNIT 1 · CONTEXT C
Changing Scotland/Britain, 1880s–present
CHANGES IN EMPLOYMENT: WOMEN

▶ **SOURCE A** *Main types of female employment, 1911 census.*

Domestic service	1,260,673
Cotton manufacture	372,834
Dressmaking	333,129
Teaching	211,183
Local government	176,450

▶ **SOURCE B** *Daily routine of housemaid, 1880:*

... to rise at six in summer and half-past six in winter; before breakfast to sweep and dust the drawing-room, dining-room, front hall and other sitting-rooms; to clean the grates and light the fires ... She makes the best beds, sweeps and dusts the rooms; cleans the grates, and lights the fires; prepares the bedrooms for the night ...

▶ **SOURCE C** First World War poster.

▶ **SOURCE D** *From a secondary text:*

With millions of men entering the armed services in 1914, women were the only remaining source of labour, and in large numbers they began taking up positions traditionally held by men in industry, farming, transport, commerce and the professions.

▶ **SOURCE E** *Clement Attlee, Deputy Prime Minister, 1942:*

The work the women are performing in munitions factories has to be seen to be believed. Precision engineering jobs which a few years ago would have made a skilled turner's hair stand on end are performed with dead accuracy by girls who had no industrial experience.

▶ **SOURCE F** *From a secondary text:*

The position of women improved in the post-war world. Nevertheless, in 1951 they tended to occupy rather inferior positions in commerce and industry, and their wages were frequently lower than those of men doing the same work. Most occupations are now in 1975 open to women, top executive posts are filled with persons of either sex, married women are able to carry on with their careers, and equal pay for equal work has been granted in many occupations.

SECTION A: KU — GENERAL

1. Describe changing jobs and career opportunities for British women between 1911 and 1940. (4)

2. Why did the range of jobs open to women increase during the twentieth century? (4)

3. How important was the question of equality in the workplace in post 1945 Britain? Explain your answer. (4)

SECTION B: EV — GEN/CREDIT

1. How reliable are Sources C and E as evidence of the importance of female labour in wartime Britain? (4)

2. To what extent do Sources D and F make similar points about women's work in twentieth century Britain? (3)

3. Do the sources provide a full and accurate picture of female employment in twentieth century Britain? Fully explain your answer. (5)

UNIT 1 · CONTEXT C
Changing Scotland/Britain, 1880s–present
CHANGES IN SOCIAL CONDITIONS: HEALTH

▶ **SOURCE A** *Adapted from a secondary text:*

Food consumption (in lbs) per head of population

	1888	1894	1901
Bacon/ham	10	13	20
Beef	9	16	21
Mutton	3	7	10
Butter	5	7	10
Eggs (number)	30	37	49
Cocoa	0.5	0.6	1.2
Tea	5	5.5	6

▶ **SOURCE B** *Working class family, 1901. Welfare worker's report:*

They cannot save nor can they join sick club or trade union. The children must have no pocket money. The father must smoke no tobacco and must drink no beer. The mother must never buy any pretty clothes. Should a child fall ill it must be attended by the parish doctor; should it die it must be buried by the parish. The wage earner must never be absent from his work.

▶ **SOURCE C** *(i) Report of a health visitor, early 1930s:*

Mrs J's husband has been out of work fourteen weeks and there's five of them starving on fifteen shillings a week. She's a young woman of 26, but she's gone away almost to a skeleton through sheer starvation. Though she was nursing a baby, I found that all the food she herself had yesterday was a cup of tea at breakfast time and tea and two slices of bread and butter, provided by a married sister living near, at tea-time. From her husband's unemployment pay of £1, five shillings had to go to pay off a debt, six shillings and threepence for rent, and only eight shillings and ninepence was left for food and fire. A school dinner for the eldest child was divided with his four-year-old brother every day and saved them from utter starvation.

(ii) Report of a charity worker, 1938:

Children very pleasant, rosy cheeks, clean white regular teeth; disproportionate amount spent on children who are neatly and sensibly clothed and appeared to be well fed ... Parents determined to do their best for them. Wife seems undernourished ...

▶ **SOURCE D** *From a novel of the 1930s called* Love on the Dole:

Next Friday or Saturday ... they would hand over their wages to Mr Price in return for whatever they had pawned today. And next Monday they would pawn again whatever they had pawned today, paying Mr Price interest on interest until they were so deep in the mire of debt that not only did Mr Price own their and their family's clothes, but also the family income as well.

SECTION A: KU — GENERAL

1 Describe possible sources of help for poor people in Britain in the 1900s and 1930s. (4)

2 What were the main causes of poverty in Britain in the 1900s and 1930s, and why was it so difficult to improve things? (5)

3 Was poverty brought about by the poor themselves or by forces outside their control? Explain your answer. (3)

SECTION B: EV — GEN/CREDIT

1 Discuss the value of Sources C and D as useful and reliable evidence of poverty in the 1930s. (4)

2 In what ways do Sources A and B appear to give differing views of living standards in Britain in the 1900s? (4)

3 Were the kinds of problem described in Sources C and D typical among working-class families in 1930s? Explain your answer. (4)

UNIT 1 · CONTEXT C ·
Changing Scotland/Britain, 1880s–present
PARLIAMETARY REFORM: EXTENSION OF FRANCHISE

The Reform Act of 1885 created a mass working class electorate.

▶ **SOURCE A** *Secret ballot (after 1872).*

▶ **SOURCE B** *Conservative MP, 1886:*

The Conservative Party will never exercise power until it has gained the confidence of the working classes; and the working classes are quite determined to govern themselves, and will not be hoodwinked by any class or class interests.

If you want to gain the confidence of the working classes let them take a real and large share in your Party councils and in your Party government.

▶ **SOURCE C**

Date	Who Voted/Constituencies
1884	All householders and lodgers paying £10 p.a. rent (boroughs and counties).
1885	Only towns bigger than 15,000 people had an MP — above 50,000 had two MPs.
1918	Vote for all men over 21 ... for women over 30. Only towns bigger than 50,000 had an MP ... Over 120,000 had two MPs.
1928	Vote for all women over 21.

Politics in the 1940s and 1960s.

▶ **SOURCE D** *The 1945 General Election.*

The Conservatives were in favour of Social reform. They had a 'Four Year Plan' for building a better Britain. They used Churchill's reputation in their election work ... The Labour party had a programme of social and economic reform ... In cinemas and halls, outside factories, in public squares candidates addressed their audiences ... The whole nation used radio. Night after night the voters listened in. They heard politicians put plans, promising, promising ...

▶ **SOURCE E** *The desire for popularity* (Daily Express *1966*).

'Marvellous! My popularity among the passengers isn't sinking!' (Prime Minister, Harold Wilson)

SECTION A: KU — GENERAL

1 In what ways did Britain become a more democratic country after 1872? (4)

2 Why did growing democracy bring about significant changes in the attitudes and organisation of political parties in Britain? (3)

3 Has growing political democracy in modern Britain brought more benefits or problems for the country? Explain your answer fully. (5)

SECTION B: EV — GEN/CREDIT

1 How useful is Source B as evidence of democratic change in Britain in the nineteenth century? (4)

2 Do Sources B and D give similar or differing accounts of the workings of popular democracy in modern Britain? Explain your answer. (4)

3 Do the sources give a reliable and fair picture of the workings of popular democracy in Britain during the twentieth century? Explain. (4)

· UNIT 1 · CONTEXT C ·
Changing Scotland/Britain, 1880s–present
HOUSING

▶ **SOURCE A** *Eye witness — Glasgow tenement about 1886:*

In some rooms may be found a jumble of articles — old beds, tables, chairs, boxes, pots and dishes, with little care for order or cleanliness. In others, a shakedown (bed) in the corner, a box or barrel for a table, a broken stool, an old pot or pan with a few dishes. In many rooms, no furniture at all, and the whole family, men, women and children, huddled together at night on such straw or rags as they can gather.

▶ **SOURCE B** *Tenement close, Dundee, 1920.*

▶ **SOURCE C** *From a secondary text:*

In 1923 Neville Chamberlain tackled the housing problem. Treasury money at the rate of £6 per house for twenty years was offered to private house-builders. He argued that this would encourage better-off families to move to new houses, leaving older houses for less well-off families to occupy. Councils were simply to provide houses for poorer people for whom no private contractor was prepared to build. The Labour Government in 1924 launched a new house-building programme, offering local councils £9 a year for each house if they would build council houses. Yet even these were too dear for many working people.

▶ **SOURCE D** *Housing in the 1930s.*

The town council acquired land and set out an avenue of houses, built in pairs or in fours, with gardens front and back. The houses varied in size from living-room and two bedrooms with bathroom, to living-room, dining-room and three bedrooms, also with bathroom and kitchen. Sometimes the sites were transformed into public parks and playing fields with enclosures for children with swings and see-saws.

SECTION A: KU — GENERAL

1. What were the main features of city tenements in Scotland in the late nineteenth/early twentieth centuries? (4)

2. What were the results of government action with regard to housing in the 1920s and 1930s? (4)

3. How important was the work of local government in housing reform in the twentieth century? Explain your answer. (4)

SECTION B: EV — GEN/CREDIT

1. How useful is Source A as evidence of Scottish housing in the late nineteenth century? (4)

2. What similarities and differences are there in the descriptions of Scottish housing given in Sources A and B? (3)

3. Does Source B or D give a more typical account of urban housing in the 1920s–30s? Fully explain and support your answer. (5)

· UNIT 1 · CONTEXT C ·
Changing Scotland/Britain, 1880s–present
POPULATION: DISTRIBUTION AND CHANGE

▶ **SOURCE A** *A Government Commission Report 1893:*

A young woman will hand over her 'kist' (box of clothes) to the porter, get her ticket for Glasgow, laugh and talk with her parents and comrades, jump into the train, pay her adieu, and thank her stars that she is at last leaving the unwomanly job (farmwork) for domestic service and town society.

▶ **SOURCE B** *From same Report:*

In 1820 to cultivate, reap and deliver five different crops would have taken 53 days, while in 1892 the same operations would be performed by those using modern methods in 35 days. The labour displaced would be one man for every 34 acres worked.

▶ **SOURCE C** *From a secondary text:*

During the century population increased threefold to four and a half millions, and, with the decline of rural industries, crowding increased in the larger towns, where slums multiplied. Conditions were little better in the industrial villages which sprang up near pits and ironworks. These were often rows of cramped houses and offered little recreation.

▶ **SOURCE D** *'Leaving for America'.*

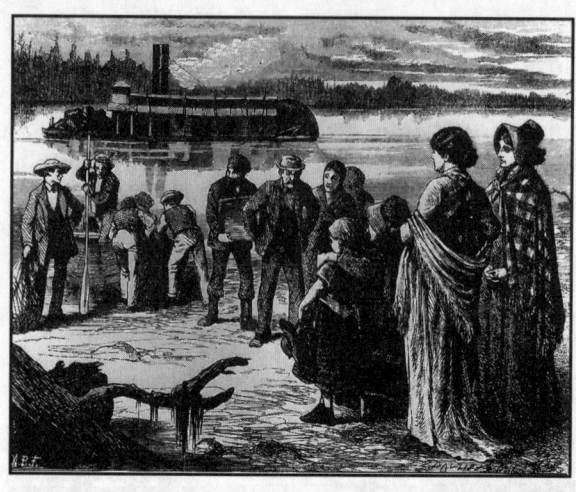

▶ **SOURCE E** *From a secondary text:*

Jealousy of the Irish migrants as incomers and as rivals for jobs combined with a revival of anti-Catholic bitterness to produce many scenes of violence. Irish men and women continued to come over, mostly for permanent work in Clyde shipyards, but some in large bands of 'tattie-howkers' for the potato harvest. At the 1901 census, the number of Catholics in Scotland was 431,900, the great majority of them being of Irish origin.

SECTION A: KU — GENERAL

1 Describe the patterns of population movement within Scotland 1880–1930. (4)

2 Explain the causes of migration in these times. (4)

3 Was the wish to better their lives the most important cause of migration among Scottish and Irish people? (4)

SECTION B: EV — GEN/CREDIT

1 How useful are Sources A and B as evidence of migration in the 1890s? (3)

2 Do Sources A, B and E give different explanations of causes of migration? (4)

3 Do the sources give an accurate explanation of migration? Explain. (5)

UNIT 1 · CONTEXT C ·
Changing Scotland/Britain, 1880s–present
EMPLOYMENT: ROLE OF TRADE UNIONS

▶**SOURCE A** *'The Farm Labourer's Song':*

Says the master to me 'Is it true? I am told
Your name on the books of the Union's enrolled
I never can allow that a workman of mine
With wicked disturbers of peace should be found

For twenty years mostly my bread has been dry
And to butter it now I shall certainly try
And though I respect you, remember I'm free
No master in England shall trample on me.

▶**SOURCE B** *From a secondary text:*

In 1889 the London dockers struck for a minimum wage of 6 pence an hour. The Port of London was paralysed for nearly a month. Their determination, as much as the hardship they suffered won them much support. Over £80,000 was subscribed to maintain the dockers' families. This was decisive and the dock owners were forced to grant the 'dockers' tanner'.

▶**SOURCE C** The Times, *Sept 1889:*

If the dock labourers and their employers had been left alone to fight it out, the workers could not have held out for a week. (But) the harsh case of the men excited the sympathy of all riverside workers. These made a compact industrial army, without whom the shipping trade of London could not proceed. More than that, the case of the dock labourers took a powerful hold on public opinion. Thus the men were placed beyond the reach of starvation. They were able to bargain on equal terms with their employer and they were successful.

▶**SOURCE D** *One man's view:*

The sole defence of the old trade unionism is its money bag, its only offensive weapon the crazy strike. Capitalism can afford to laugh at both.

▶**SOURCE E** *From a secondary text:*

In the early twentieth century further advances were made and great alliances of miners, railwaymen and transport workers were formed to organise combined action.

SECTION A: KU — GENERAL

1 What were the main developments in British trade unionism 1880–1914? (4)

2 Why was there increasing industrial tension during the 1880–1914 period? (4)

3 How important was the 1889 Dock Strike in the development of trade unionism? (4)

SECTION B: EV — GEN/CREDIT

1 How useful are Sources A and C as evidence on trade unions in the 1880s? (5)

2 Explain the different points of view put forward in Sources C and D. (4)

3 How typical were the views put forward in Source D in the 1880s? (3)

UNIT 1 · CONTEXT C ·
Changing Scotland/Britain, 1880s–present
CREDIT LEVEL — KU QUESTIONS

1 *The last 100 years have seen persistent migration within Britain and from Britain to other countries.*

Discuss the causes of either migration within Britain or emigration from Scotland during the period from 1880 to the present day. (4)

2 *An industrial enquiry of 1966 concluded that there were too many shipyards in Britain and that these were too small.*

Describe the main changes affecting British shipbuilding during the twentieth century. (4)

3 *Scotland faced serious social and health problems after 1918. Housing was poor — 48 per cent of Scots people lived in one or two-roomed houses compared with 7 per cent in England.*

To what extent can Scotland's health problems in the twentieth century be explained by inadequate housing for its people? (4)

4 *The position improved in post-1945 Britain but, from the 1951 Census, it was clear that British women still tended to occupy inferior positions in commerce and industry.*

Explain how changing employment opportunities in twentieth century Britain have affected women. (4)

5 *Choose either question A or question B.*

A *At the close of the nineteenth century the Liberal and Conservative Parties had fixed attachments to the upper and middle classes of society. The workers felt that their views were inadequately represented.*

How important has increasing working-class political influence been in the development of democracy in Britain from the 1880s to the present time? (8)
For this question you should write a short essay of several paragraphs.

B *'The argument of the broken window-pane is the most valuable argument in modern politics.'*

Did female political rights come about through the efforts of campaigners for the cause, or as a result of broader changes in British society? (8)
For this question you should write a short essay of several paragraphs.

UNIT 2 · CONTEXT A ·
International Cooperation & Conflict, 1790s–1820s
CAUSES OF REVOLUTIONARY WAR, 1792–93

Between 1792 and 1793 events in France provoked general European war.

▶ **SOURCE A** *From a secondary text:*

The Edict of Fraternity of November 1792 promised help to people who rose against their rulers ... It was a challenge to every Government in Europe. Moreover, the French revolutionary Government while thus appealing to the subjects of foreign rulers resented any action of foreigners in support of the French King. The truth was that the new order in France and the old order in the rest of Europe were totally opposed. Conflict was inevitable.

▶ **SOURCE B** *Robespierre, writing in 1793:*

What is our aim? It is to use the Constitution for the good of the people. What are the obstacles to the achievement of freedom? The war at home and abroad. By what means can the foreign war be ended? By placing Republican generals at the head of our armies and by punishing those who have betrayed us. How can we end the Civil War? By punishing traitors ... and by making terrible examples of those who have stood against liberty and spilt the blood of patriots.

▶ **SOURCE C** *From a secondary text:*

The rulers of Europe began to draw together. After the execution of Louis on 21st January 1793, the French Ambassador in London was dismissed, and the French Revolutionary Convention declared war against Britain and Holland on 1st February and against Spain in March. Thus was formed a great alliance — the First Coalition — of Austria, Prussia, Sardinia, Britain, Holland and Spain against France. When the campaign of 1793 opened, therefore, France was face-to-face with the whole of Europe. Would the Allies push on vigorously before France had time to recover stability and organise her resources? The answer to that question would determine the ultimate issue of the war, and for that reason 1793 was the critical period of the war. In the early part of the year, the French lost ground heavily, but, by the autumn the effect of organisation and enthusiasm was making itself felt, and the tide began to turn.

▶ **SOURCE D** *Call from the French Government, August 1793:*

From this moment on until the enemies have been driven out of the territory of the French Republic, all French people are permanently enlisted for the service of the armies. Young men will go and fight; married men will forge arms and transport supplies; the women will make tents and clothes and will serve in the hospitals; children will make old linen into bandages; old men will teach hatred of kings and build republican unity.

SECTION A: KU — GENERAL

1 What were the aims of the revolutionary leaders in France? (4)

2 For what reasons was there general European war by 1793? Explain your answer fully. (5)

3 Was it the intention of the revolutionary leaders to defend France or to spread revolutionary ideas across Europe? Briefly explain. (3)

SECTION B: EV — GEN/CREDIT

1 How useful are Sources B and D as reliable evidence about attitudes of French people in 1793? (4)

2 What similar ideas are put forward in Sources B and D? (4)

3 How significant is Source D in explaining developments in France after 1793? Explain. (4)

UNIT 2 · CONTEXT A ·
International Cooperation & Conflict, 1790s–1820s
COALITIONS AGAINST FRANCE: RUSSIAN CAMPAIGN

Napoleon's attitude towards Russia, his ally of 1807, changed after that date.

▶ **SOURCE A** *Napoleon writing to his Foreign Minister, 1807:*

I will meet with the Central European leaders at Erfurt and wish to come back free to do what I want in Spain. I want to be sure that Austria will be contained, and I do not want to be involved in any specific way in the East. Prepare for me an agreement which will satisfy Tsar Alexander and which is, above all, directed against England and with which I can feel at ease.

▶ **SOURCE B** *Napoleon to his Foreign Minister, 1812:*

Imagine Moscow taken, Russia overthrown, the Tsar either forced to accept defeat or perhaps murdered by a palace plot. A new and dependent throne for us. And tell me if it is not then possible for a large army of Frenchmen and auxiliaries to leave Russia by the southern route through Tiflis and reach the Ganges and India... A touch of a French sword is all that is needed for the framework of English trading greatness to collapse.

The French invasion of Russia was a spectacular failure.

▶ **SOURCE C** *From a secondary text:*

He had waited too long in Moscow. Fresh Russian armies barred the southern route home and the French were forced back on the route that had been laid waste on the march east. Though October was quite mild and November too, the lack of food and constant harassment of the Cossacks made the retreat a nightmare... Only the famous Imperial Guard held the French army together... With December came terrible cold, with frosts of 30 degrees. What was left of the army became a desperate rabble. On 6th December, Napoleon hurried away by coach for Paris, and eight days later Marshall Ney... crossed the Niemen with less than a sixteenth of the original army. 'General Famine and General Winter' wrote Ney to his wife, 'rather than Russian bullets, have conquered the Grand Army.' What he might have added, but did not, was General Bonaparte's terrible over-confidence and miscalculations.

▶ **SOURCE D** *British cartoon, 1812.*

'If you trespass on our ground you must dance to our tunes.' (Russian peasants)

SECTION A: KU — GENERAL

1 How did Napoleon's plans for military advance in Europe and beyond change between 1807 and 1812? (4)

2 For what reasons was Napoleon particularly concerned with Russia and Britain? (4)

3 Was Napoleon's over-confidence the most important reason for the failure of the French campaign in Russia? Briefly explain. (4)

SECTION B: EV — GEN/CREDIT

1 How useful are Sources A and B as evidence of Napoleon's actions as a statesman? (4)

2 In what ways do Sources C and D put forward similar or different ideas about the French campaign in Russia in 1812? (3)

3 Do the sources accurately show Napoleon's importance in events in Europe between 1807 and 1812? Explain your answer fully. (5)

UNIT 2 · CONTEXT B ·
International Cooperation & Conflict, 1890s–1920s
GREAT POWER ALLIANCES

▶ **SOURCE A** *Great Power comparisons, 1914.*

ENTENTE	Britain	France	Russia
Population	45M	40M	164M
Land forces	711,000	1,250,000	1,200,000
Arms spending	£50M	£37M	£67M
Battleships	64	28	16

CENTRAL POWERS	Germany	Austria-Hun
Population	65M	50M
Land forces	2,200,000	810,000
Arms spending	£60M	£22M
Battleships	49	16

▶ **SOURCE B** *Alliances by 1914.*

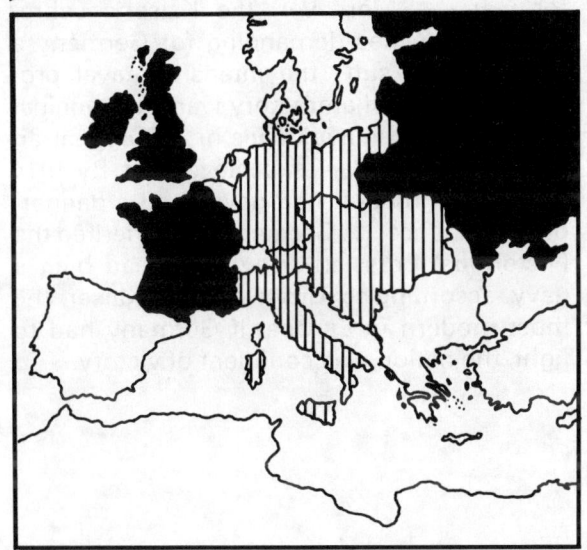

▶ **SOURCE C** *Adapted from a secondary text:*

The international scene was changed by the eclipse of Russia, the emergence of Germany and the Entente. Grey (British Foreign Secretary) was determined to stand by France. He was impatient to see Russia re-established in European politics. He looked forward to an agreement with Russia that would extend the Entente with France. He wanted friendly relations with Germany provided Germany accepted Britain's friendly relations with France and Russia.

Comments on the European international scene.

▶ **SOURCE D** *British Colonial Secretary, 1912:*

The assumption that we are in fact members of a new Triple Alliance, opposed to the old (i.e. the Triple Alliance of Germany, Austria and Italy), is so mischievous and dangerous that I think some early opportunity should be taken of making it clear to both France and Russia that such an assumption is wholly opposed to our policy and intentions.

▶ **SOURCE E** *An American observer, 1914:*

The situation is extraordinary. It is militarism run stark mad. Unless someone can bring about a different understanding there is some day to be an awful catastrophe. No one in Europe can do it. There is too much hatred, too many jealousies. When England consents, France and Russia will close on Germany and Austria.

SECTION A: KU — GENERAL

1 What made Europe an increasingly dangerous place in the years before 1914? (4)

2 To what extent did the results of military and diplomatic developments before 1914 give a seeming advantage to the Entente Powers? (4)

3 How important was Britain's role in Europe in the years before 1914? (4)

SECTION B: EV — GEN/CREDIT

1 How reliable is Source D as evidence of British Government attitudes towards Europe? (3)

2 In what ways are the ideas put forward in Sources D and E similar or different? Explain. (4)

3 Does Source D or Source E give the more convincing explanation of the European situation before 1914? Fully explain. (5)

UNIT 2 · CONTEXT B
International Cooperation & Conflict, 1890s–1920s
TENSION — NAVAL RACE

Britain and Germany: naval rivalry

▶ **SOURCE A** *The Kaiser in the* Daily Telegraph *interview, 1908:*

'But,' you will say, 'what of the German Navy? Surely that is a menace to England?' ... My answer is clear. ... Germany is a young and growing Empire. She has a world-wide trade which is rapidly expanding. Germany must have a powerful fleet to protect that trade in even the most distant seas.... Only those Powers which have great navies will be listened to with respect when the future of the Pacific comes to be solved. England indeed may be glad that Germany has a fleet when they speak together on the same side in the great debates of the future.

▶ **SOURCE B** *Ex First Sea Lord Fisher, 1912:*

Every petty German newspaper is dead-on for war with England! So anything would kindle a war.

Hence the pith of Winston's speech lies in the words: 'We must be ready to meet at our average moment anything an enemy might hurl at us at his selected moment.'

▶ **SOURCE C** *Dreadnought Race.*

	Britain	Germany
1906	1	0
1907	3	0
1908	2	4
1909	2	3
1910	3	1
1911	5	3
1912	3	2
1913	7	3
1914	3	1

▶ **SOURCE D** *Adapted from a secondary text:*

German prosperity was based on preparation for war. ... Moreover, the Kaiser's sabre-rattling speeches demanding for Germany a 'place in the sun', the intensive naval programme, and inflammatory warnings against Russia made the avoidance of war appear an accident rather than an achievement. By 1914 the German nation had developed a dangerous confidence.... Germany had inherited the (victorious) Prussian army. ... It had built a navy, according to Tirpitz and the Kaiser, the most modern in Europe. If Germany had to fight, the nation was confident of victory.

SECTION A: KU — GENERAL

1 What did the Kaiser do to try to improve relations between Germany and Britain in the years before 1914? (4)

2 What were the main causes of worsening British-German relations? (4)

3 Was war between Britain and Germany inevitable and unavoidable? Explain. (4)

SECTION B: EV — GEN/CREDIT

1 Would people in Britain be likely to be convinced by the arguments put forward in Source A? Explain your answer. (4)

2 To what extent do Sources A and D give differing accounts of German naval policy before 1914? (4)

3 How significant are the sources in explaining the nature and cause of growing tensions between Britain and Germany before 1914? (4)

UNIT 2 · CONTEXT B ·
International Cooperation & Conflict, 1890s–1920s
SARAJEVO — OUTBREAK OF WAR

▶ **SOURCE A** *From a secondary text:*

The idea of the assassination of the Archduke seems to have come from some students who belonged to the movement 'Young Bosnia', a pro-Slav organisation dedicated to the overthrow of Austrian rule. Princip, a nineteen-year-old student, and some colleagues obtained weapons. Arms and facilities for crossing the Bosnian border were supplied by the Black Hand Society, headed by Serbia's military intelligence chief. The Serbian Prime Minister received a report on the movement of the assassins. On 28th June Princip shot the Archduke and his wife.

▶ **SOURCE B** *Adapted from a letter from Austria to Serbia, 23 July:*

It became clear, from the evidence of the criminal authors of the outrage of 28 June, that the murder at Sarajevo was thought up in Belgrade (Serbian capital), that the murderers received arms and bombs from Serbian (army) officers and officials... and that transportation of the criminals and their arms was arranged by Serbian border officials.

▶ **SOURCE C** *Adapted from the Serbian reply, 25 July:*

The Royal Serbian Government considers it a duty to begin an enquiry against all who are, or who might be implicated in the 28 June plot. It cannot accept participation in this enquiry of Austro-Hungarian authorities (as Austria demanded)...

▶ **SOURCE D** *From a secondary text:*

Russia could not allow Serbia to be humiliated. Now the Russians found that if they mobilised against Austria they would be defenceless against Germany. General mobilisation was their only course. On 30 July, they resolved upon it. The Russian decision to mobilise threw out the German timetable. If the Germans did nothing they would have to fight a war on two fronts, not on one. On 31 July the German Chancellor asked the Military Chief of Staff, 'Is the Fatherland in danger?' Moltke answered, 'Yes'. This was the moment of decision. Germany sent an ultimatum demanding Russian demobilization within twelve hours. On 1 August Germany declared war on Russia.

▶ **SOURCE E** *From a secondary text:*

The chief objects of Russian and French policy could be realised only through a general European war. When the assassination came the French and Russians recognised that the impending clash between Austria and Serbia would provide an appropriate episode over which to bring about the desired conflict. In estimating the order of guilt of the various countries involved, we may safely say that the only direct and immediate responsibility for World War One falls upon Serbia, France and Russia.

SECTION A: KU — GENERAL

1 In what ways were the assassins of the Austrian Archduke given assistance in their task? (4)

2 Why did the assassinations lead finally to war between Russia and Germany? Explain your answer. (4)

3 How important was German fear of Russia as an underlying cause of war? Explain your answer. (4)

SECTION B: EV — GEN/CREDIT

1 How useful are Sources B and C as evidence of Austrian and Serbian attitudes to the assassinations at Sarajevo? (4)

2 Do Sources A and B make similar or different points about how the assassinations came about? (3)

3 How accurately do Sources D and E explain how and why war spread across Europe? Fully explain your answer. (5)

· UNIT 2 · CONTEXT B ·
International Cooperation & Conflict, 1890s–1920s
EXPERIENCE OF WAR: TECHNOLOGY

▶ **SOURCE A** *An artist's view of the trenches.*

▶ **SOURCE B** *From a secondary text:*

In 1914 troops on the Western Front dug ditches and sheltered in them from enemy fire. Later they made deeper and wider trenches. Second and third lines of trenches were dug with others connecting these lines. In front of the first trenches were laid tangled masses of barbed wire. Beyond lay No Man's Land ... In an attack the enemy lines were subjected to heavy artillery bombardment before the troops went over the top ... Sometimes a few hundred yards of trenches were captured, but counter-attacks could be launched from further back and the stalemate was resumed.

▶ **SOURCE C** *Stretcher-bearer Frank Dunham:*

On still nights we could hear Fritz walking on his duckboards and talking with his comrades. Being on sentry duty was far from being a pleasant job as often without warning a machine-gun would play on the parapet, necessitating 'ducking' to prevent being hit ...

▶ **SOURCE D** *Soldier George Coppard:*

Some of the leading tanks carried huge bundles of tightly-bound brushwood ... It was pretty marvellous to know that for one precious hour the tanks had borne the brunt of the attack and not us. We went forward into enemy country in a manner never possible without the aid of tanks ... It was broad daylight as we crossed No Man's Land and the German front-line. I saw few wounded coming back. The tanks appeared to have busted through any resistance. The enemy wire had been dragged about like old curtains, though it was not comparable in density to the terrible wire at the beginning of the Somme battle.

SECTION A: KU — GENERAL

1 Describe the normal layout of trench systems on the western front in the First World War. (4)

2 Why did both sides in the war find it extremely difficult to break out from their defensive positions and advance into enemy territory? (4)

3 How important was the introduction of the tank on the western front in the First World War? Explain your answer. (4)

SECTION B: EV — GEN/CREDIT

1 How reliable are Sources A and C as evidence of trench warfare on the western front? (4)

2 Do Sources A and C provide similar or different accounts of trench warfare from that given in Source B? Explain your answer. (4)

3 Are the experiences described in Sources C and D typical of the experiences of most soldiers on the western front? Explain your answer. (4)

UNIT 2 · CONTEXT B ·
International Cooperation & Conflict, 1890s–1920s
EXPERIENCE OF WAR — CIVILIAN LIFE

Anti-German propaganda was issued during the First World War.

▶ **SOURCE A** *A war poem, by a twelve-year-old girl:*

> Down with the Germans,
> Down with them all.
> Oh Army and Navy,
> Be sure of their fall.
> Spare not one of them.
> Those deceitful spies.
> Cut their tongues,
> Pull out their eyes.
> Down with them all.

▶ **SOURCE B** *An American recruitment poster.*

▶ **SOURCE C** *Army poster.*

4 QUESTIONS to men who have not enlisted

1. IF you are physically fit and between 19 and 38 years of age, are you really satisfied with what you are doing to-day?
2. Do you feel happy as you walk along the streets and see other men wearing the King's uniform?
3. What will you say in years to come when people ask you "Where did you serve in the great War"?
4. What will you answer when your children grow up and say, "Father, why weren't you a soldier, too"?

ENLIST TO-DAY.

Food shortages in wartime Britain

▶ **SOURCE D** *From a secondary text:*

As many as one million people were standing weekly in the London area alone, waiting hour after hour for food which was often all gone before their turn came. On 21 January 1918 'The queues at Smithfield meat market were very large: at 11 o'clock one queue consisted of 4,000 people.' And on 25 January 'There were butter and margarine queues, and, a new development, fish queues.'

▶ **SOURCE E** *Wartime British poster.*

SECTION A: KU — GENERAL

1 In what ways were men encouraged to join the armed forces during the First World War? (4)

2 Why did the government try to change people's eating habits during the First World War? (3)

3 How important was it for the warring countries to organise the home front as well as win victories on the war front? Fully explain your answer. (5)

SECTION B: EV — GEN/CREDIT

1 To what extent are Sources C and E useful evidence of how the authorities tried to influence people's lives in wartime Britain? (4)

2 To what extent do Sources A and B give similar views of Germany and Germans? (4)

3 How significant are the sources in showing the changing effects of the war on the home front in Britain? (4)

· UNIT 2 · CONTEXT B ·
International Cooperation & Conflict, 1890s–1920s
TREATY OF VERSAILLES

▶ **SOURCE A** *British Prime Minister Lloyd George, on the Versailles Treaty, July 1919:*

In 1914 you had a German Empire which possessed the greatest army in the world ... It was the terror of the world ... It has now been reduced to a force unable to disturb the peace of the weakest of her neighbours ... There was a navy, the second in the world ... Where is it now? ... The colonies of Germany covered about one and a half million square miles. Stripped of the lot! ... The ruler who spoke for her pride and her majesty and her might — now a fugitive — is soon to be placed on trial ... Her war debt more than doubled to pay for reparations.

▶ **SOURCE B** *War guilt clause, Versailles Treaty:*

The Allied and Associated Governments affirm the responsibility of Germany in causing all the loss and damage to which they and their citizens have been subjected as a result of the war imposed upon them by German aggression.

▶ **SOURCE C** *Comments of Allied leaders during Versailles peace talks:*

When Germany defeated France in 1870 she made France pay. That is the principle we shall proceed upon.

We'll get out of Germany all that you can get out of a lemon and a bit more. I would squeeze her until you can hear the pips squeak.

▶ **SOURCE D** *A cartoon of 1919.*

The Tiger: "Curious! I seem to hear a child weeping!"

▶ **SOURCE E** *From a secondary text:*

The war had changed the map of Europe. New nation-states had appeared. The talk might be about hanging the Kaiser and making Germany pay. The real issues were different: how to rebuild a peaceful world, substituting the security of a collective will to peace for the security of arms and military alliances. There was the opportunity for a new beginning, not least because of the intervention of the USA in the affairs of Europe. The experiment failed and in the thirties the divisions between the major powers in Europe were sadly reminiscent of 1913. The failure began in Paris in 1919.

SECTION A: KU — GENERAL

1 In what ways was Germany weakened by the Versailles Treaty? (4)

2 To what extent was the wish to punish Germany the main aim of the Allies during the peace talks? (4)

3 What was the importance of the war guilt clause for the people of Germany and for the Allies? (4)

SECTION B: EV — GEN/CREDIT

1 How useful is Source A as evidence of attitudes towards Germany in 1919? (4)

2 To what extent do Sources A, B and C put forward similar intentions towards Germany on the part of the Allies? (4)

3 How accurate are the sources in showing the real effects of the 1919 peace settlement in Europe? (4)

· UNIT 2 · CONTEXT B ·
International Cooperation & Conflict, 1890s–1920s
PEACE SETTLEMENT

▶ **SOURCE A** Punch *cartoon*.

President Wilson to American Eagle 'Gee, what a dove I've made you.'

▶ **SOURCE B** *From a secondary text:*

There was complete silence as the President spoke. He said that the policies of the Imperial German Government made it impossible for the USA not to enter the war.

'Vessels of every kind, whatever their flag, their cargo, their destination, have ruthlessly been sent to the bottom without warning and without thought of help for those on board, the vessels of friendly neutrals along with those of belligerents ... The world must be made safe for democracy!'

In a reference to the Zimmermann telegram he said that the German Government 'means to stir up enemies against us at our very own doors'. The roar of enthusiasm at the end of his address was echoed by the whole nation.

▶ **SOURCE C** *President Wilson in a speech made at the end of the war:*

There is a great tide running in the hearts of men. The hearts of men have never been so singularly in unison before. Men have never been so conscious of their brotherhood. It will be our privilege, I believe, to make Right and Justice the controlling forces in the world.

▶ **SOURCE D** *From a secondary text:*

By April 1919 Wilson was exhausted. He had constant bouts of 'flu and left Europe as soon as the Germans accepted the dictated Versailles Treaty on 28th June ... He took the draft of the Treaty to the Senate. The Senators rejected it ... Later on during 1920 he tried to turn the Presidential Election into a referendum on the League of Nations. Harding, the Republican candidate, opposed US entry into the League ... The electors had to choose between Wilson's world involvement and Harding's policy of 'isolation'. They chose Harding and rejected membership of the League.

SECTION A: KU — GENERAL

1. Describe the role of the USA during and after the First World War. (4)

2. Why did the USA enter the war? (4)

3. How important were the actions of President Wilson for the future of his own country and for Europe and the world? (4)

SECTION B: EV — GEN/CREDIT

1. Are Sources A and C useful and reliable as evidence on the attitudes and policies of President Wilson? Explain your answer. (4)

2. To what extent do Sources A and B appear to give differing views of the US leader? (4)

3. How accurate are the sources in summing up the successes and failures of President Wilson? (4)

UNIT 2 · CONTEXT B ·
International Cooperation & Conflict, 1890s–1920s
LEAGUE OF NATIONS — SECURITY

▶SOURCE A *From the Covenant of the Leagues of Nations, 1919:*

Any war or threat of war, is hereby declared a matter of concern to the whole League, and the League shall take any action that may be deemed wise and effectual to safeguard the peace of nations.

Should any member of the League resort to war in disregard of its covenants, it shall be deemed to have committed an act of war against all other members of the League, which hereby undertake to subject it to the severance of all trade or financial relations.

The Council of the League shall recommend what effective military, naval or air force the members of the League shall contribute to the armed forces to be used to protect the covenants of the League.

▶SOURCE B *President Wilson in 1919:*

There is a great tide running in the hearts of men. Men have never been so conscious of their brotherhood. It will be our privilege, I believe, to make Right and Justice the controlling forces in the world.

▶SOURCE C *US politician Theodore Roosevelt in a speech of 1919:*

Mr Wilson has no authority to speak for the American people. His Fourteen Points and all his utterances every which way have ceased to be accepted as expressing the will of the American people.

▶SOURCE D *From a secondary text:*

Without USA and Russia the League was not a truly world-wide organisation, though its membership was numerically impressive. In Japan and Italy it had two leading members intent on pursuing their own expansionist ambitions regardless of the effect this would have on the League or world peace. Britain and France tried to steer the League in opposing directions. While the French sought to strengthen League obligations and make these more binding on member states, Britain was concerned that use of economic sanctions would only result in further loss of trade. Military and naval measures might lead to confrontation with the USA and would add to Britain's considerable military burden.

SECTION A: KU — GENERAL

1 How did the League of Nations intend to maintain international peace? (4)

2 Why did the League come into being in 1919? (3)

3 How important was non-membership of the USA in the activities of the League in the 1920s? Fully explain your answer. (5)

SECTION B: EV — GEN/CREDIT

1 How useful are Sources B and C as evidence of US attitudes to peace? (4)

2 Do Sources A and B agree on the principles of the League of Nations? Explain your answer. (4)

3 Were the points of view expressed in Source B typical among world leaders in 1919? Explain your answer. (4)

UNIT 2 · CONTEXT B ·
International Cooperation and Conflict, 1890s–1920s
CREDIT LEVEL — KU QUESTIONS

1 *'The situation is militarism run stark mad ... There is some day to be an awful catastrophe.'*
(An American observer on European international tension in 1913–14)

Why did war in Europe appear to many to be inevitable in the period 1908–1914? (4)

2 *The assassin's pistol shots on 28 June 1914 were called by one observer 'The shots that rang around the world.'*

Describe the events that followed the assassination of Franz Ferdinand and his wife in Sarajevo and which led to general war. (4)

3 *Answer either question A or question B.*

A *We are the dead. Short days ago, we lived, felt dawn, saw sunset glow. Loved and were loved, and now we lie, in Flanders field.*

Why did war on the western front result in appalling and unprecedented casualties and loss of life? (8)
For this question you should write a short essay of several paragraphs.

B *Total war involved all citizens, civilian as well as military.*

To what extent was the First World War a 'total war' involving everyone living in the countries involved? (8)
For this question you should write a short essay of several paragraphs.

4 *While the tank and the aeroplane made their first appearance in war, it was weapons of an earlier date — the rifle, the artillery cannon, and the machine-gun — which were the most decisive.*

Describe the changing technology of war on the western front during the First World War. (4)

2 *'We will get out of Germany all that you can get out of a lemon and a bit more.'*
(Lloyd George talking about peace negotiations with defeated Germany in 1919)

How important to the outcome of the Versailles Treaty was the desire of the victors to punish and weaken Germany? (4)

6 *'It will be our privilege to make Right and Justice the controlling forces in the world'*
(Woodrow Wilson in 1919)

To what extent did the League of Nations succeed in bringing right and justice into international affairs during the 1920s? (4)

UNIT 2 · CONTEXT C ·
International Cooperation & Conflict, 1930s–1960s
GERMAN REARMAMENT AFTER 1933

▶ **SOURCE A** *From a secondary text:*

On March 16, 1935, Hitler decreed a law establishing universal military service and providing for a peacetime army of roughly half a million men. That was the end of the military restrictions of Versailles. As Hitler expected, Britain and France protested, but took no action. March 17 was a day of celebration in Germany. The shackles of Versailles, symbol of Germany's defeat and humiliation, had been torn off. No matter how much a German might dislike Hitler and his gangster rule, to most Germans the nation's honour had been restored.

▶ **SOURCE B** *Hitler speaking in May 1935:*

National Socialist Germany wants peace because of its deep principles. No war would be likely to alter the distress in Europe. Germany needs and desires peace! We finally renounced all claims to Alsace-Lorraine for which we have fought two great wars. Germany has concluded a non-aggression pact with Poland. We shall adhere to this unconditionally. Germany neither intends nor wishes to annex Austria.

▶ **SOURCE C** *Hitler speaking in 1936:*

German and Italian rearmament is proceeding much more rapidly than rearmament in Great Britain, where it is not only a case of producing ships, guns, and aeroplanes, but also of undertaking psychological rearmament which is much longer and more difficult. In three years Germany will be ready, in four years more than ready; if five years are given, better still...

▶ **SOURCE D** *American cartoon, 1933.*

SECTION A: KU — GENERAL

1. How was German military power restored in the 1930s? (4)

2. Why was Hitler able to rearm Germany without interference from opponents? (4)

3. How important was rearmament to the German people? Explain your answer. (4)

SECTION B: EV — GEN/CREDIT

1. How did the cartoonist in Source D view Hitler? Explain your answer. (3)

2. To what extent do Sources B, C and D give consistently similar views of Hitler? (5)

3. Is Source D an accurate prediction of what was to come? Explain. (4)

UNIT 2 · CONTEXT C
International Cooperation & Conflict, 1930s–1960s
CZECH CRISIS 1938

▶ **SOURCE A** *From a secondary text:*

Chamberlain persuaded Dr Benes, the Czech leader, to agree to transfer to Germany those parts of Sudetenland where the majority of the population was German. On 22nd September Chamberlain offered Hitler the deal. ... He wanted the whole of Sudetenland ... 'How horrible, incredible, that we should be digging trenches and trying on gas-masks here because of a quarrel in a far away country between people of whom we know nothing', Chamberlain broadcast on the BBC ... He flew to Munich for talks with Hitler ... The Czechs were excluded from the talks ... On 30th September the decision was announced. Hitler was to have the whole of Sudetenland; he promised he had no more demands in Europe ... the Czechs, betrayed and isolated had to agree. The crisis was solved.

▶ **SOURCE B** *Chamberlain and French Premier Daladier, direct Nazi advance in Europe (Russian cartoon of 1938).*

▶ **SOURCE C** *Winston Churchill, September 1938:*

£1 was demanded at the pistol's point. When it was given, £2 was demanded at the pistol's point. Finally the Dictator consented to take £1 17 shillings and 6 pence and the rest in promises of goodwill for the future.

▶ **SOURCE D** *From a secondary text:*

In 1933 the Head of the British Foreign Office predicted that the new German Chancellor Hitler would proceed to tear up the clauses of the Treaty of Versailles ... and embark on a campaign of eastern expansion. The British Government had ample warning of the likely course of events but did not succeed in preventing Hitler engulfing ... Europe in war in 1939. The failure of the architects of the 1919 peace settlement to complete their work ... was a major factor contributing to the outbreak of war twenty years later.

SECTION A: KU — GENERAL

1 What was the Czechoslovakian Crisis of 1938 and how was it resolved? (4)

2 What were the reasons for British and French failure to prevent German territorial advances in Europe? (4)

3 Was war unavoidable in 1939? Explain your answer clearly. (4)

SECTION B: EV — GEN/CREDIT

1 Is Source B reliable evidence of British and French attitudes and actions in 1938? (3)

2 In what sense does Source A support the point of view expressed by the writer of Source C? (4)

3 To what extent do Sources B, C and D accurately explain the underlying causes of the Second World War. Fully explain your answer. (5)

· UNIT 2 · CONTEXT C ·
International Cooperation & Conflict, 1930s–1960s
EXPERIENCE OF WAR: CIVILIAN LIFE

Total war involved all citizens, civilian as well as military.

▶ **SOURCE A** *HM Government guide.*

ENEMY INVASION.

WHAT YOU MUST DO.

Remain at work: when unable to do so and you have no invasion duty

CONTACT YOUR LOCAL WARDEN.

He will arrange for you to help the City to carry on.

If you are in Civil Defence, that is your job.

If you have no invasion duty, stand firm.

Do not leave your district; do not block the roads.

Do not listen to rumours; only obey orders given by the military, police, Civil Defence personnel or Ministry of Information.

Be on your guard against Fifth Columnists.

Apply to your local Warden for more detailed instructions.

Keep by you a 48 hours' supply of food and water.

Issued by the Birmingham Invasion Committee.

▶ **SOURCE B** *Home Guard volunteer:*

Several of us had been in the Great War and knew how to use a rifle ... and we would have fought although our equipment wasn't very good. In my platoon we were a mixed bunch — a solicitor and two bus-drivers, while our officer was a retired tea-planter.

▶ **SOURCE C** *Wartime photograph.*

▶ **SOURCE D** *Eye-witness memory:*

Many locals complained about their evacuees and called them dirty and bad-mannered. I used to ask them how they would like to be pushed out of their houses and put in a stranger's house miles away. Those evacuees were good children — although some of them were a bit rough. Our places weren't bombed but some of theirs were. The trouble was that some of our villagers didn't want to know that there was a war on.

SECTION A: KU — GENERAL

1 Describe the measures taken both by the authorities and by individual people, to cope with enemy bombing. (5)

2 Explain the effects of heavy bombing on the people and communities of Britain. (4)

3 How important was the Home Guard in protecting the home front during the war? (3)

SECTION B: EV — GEN/CREDIT

1 How useful are Sources B and D as evidence of people's response to war within Britain? (4)

2 Compare Sources C and D as evidence of the effect of war on people in Britain. (4)

3 Do the sources realistically show the tensions and anxieties of people in wartime Britain? Explain your answer. (4)

· UNIT 2 · CONTEXT C ·
International Cooperation & Conflict, 1930s–1960s
NEW TECHNOLOGY: EFFECTS ON WAR

▶ **SOURCE A** *From* Guinness Book of Records: *Second World War casualties, costs:*

Total number of fatalities, (all
    countries)   54,800,000
    (includes 6 million Jews, 4 million
    Poles killed in war and prisons)
Total war costs to Britain   £34,423,000
    (Note: costs over five times greater than
    the First World War costs)
Total war costs to Soviet
    Union   £100,000,000,000

▶ **SOURCE B** *Adapted from a secondary text:*

The people of Hiroshima had no idea of what had hit them. They did not know that atomic bombs existed. Those who were below the centre of the blast were burnt or vapourised and ceased to exist. It has been estimated that at least 80,000 were killed. For many there was a new danger. After the explosion radioactive dust settled in the city. Radiation sickness followed for hundreds of people ... The huge fires, the howling wind and the black rain were the opening of the Atomic Age ... Overhead in the Superfortress the airmen looked down on the gigantic mushroom-shaped cloud ... One of them said, 'My God. What have we done?'

Two comments on the Hiroshima and Nagasaski attacks:

▶ **SOURCE C** *US President Truman, 1945:*

The atom bomb was no 'great decision' ... There were more people killed by fire bombs in Tokyo. The atom bomb was merely another powerful weapon in the arsenal of righteousness. The dropping of the bomb stopped the war — saved millions of lives ... It was a purely military decision to end the war.

▶ **SOURCE D** *Comment by historian, A. J. P. Taylor:*

Few foresaw the enormous increase in potential nuclear destruction which would follow within a few years. Practically no one imagined that any country except the USA would be able to develop atomic bombs in the near future. Practically no one reflected on the contaminated fall-out which would follow a nuclear explosion. War suspended morality. In wartime men are deliberately killed and maimed, and from this it was an easy step to killing and maiming future generations. Nuclear weapons were 'just another big bomb'.

▶ **SOURCE E** *Protest song on the nuclear arms race:*

To be or not to be; that is the question,
And the answer to it all ain't military datum,
Like who gets there fastest with the mostest
    atoms.
But the people of the world must decide their
    fate.
We gotta stick together or disintegrate.
We hold these truths to be self-evident:
    All men could be cremated equal.

SECTION A: KU — GENERAL

1 Describe the human and materials costs brought about by the Second World War. (4)

2 Explain the immediate and long-term effects of the nuclear attack on Hiroshima. (4)

3 How important was the invention of the atomic bomb in the development of the post-war world? Explain your answer. (4)

SECTION B: EV — GEN/CREDIT

1 How useful is Source C as evidence of attitudes towards nuclear warfare in USA at the end of the war? (4)

2 Compare the points of view on nuclear warfare put forward in Sources C and D. (4)

3 Are the views put forward in Source E typical of popular attitudes towards the development of nuclear weapons in the post-war period? Explain your answer. (4)

UNIT 2 · CONTEXT C
International Cooperation & Conflict, 1930s–1960s
BRITAIN, USA, USSR AFTER 1945

Britain's status changed after the Second World War.

▶ **SOURCE A** *A British cartoon, 1943.*

▶ **SOURCE B** *From a secondary text:*

By 1949, the right of colonies to self-government was now backed by the fact that the main colonial powers were exhausted from their efforts in the Second World War. In the post-war years many colonies were therefore able to gain their independence ... With Britain, most of these countries remained in the Commonwealth. By these developments, coupled with the already 'grown up' status of the great dominions of Canada, Australia and New Zealand, the Commonwealth became a far less powerful organisation.

Britain as a world power in the 1960s

▶ **SOURCE C** *From a secondary text:*

In February 1959 British Prime Minister Macmillan went to Moscow and obtained Kruschev's agreement to a (nuclear) test ban treaty. Tripartite discussions were then held between Britain, USA and USSR ... In 1963 Macmillan persuaded the Russians and Americans that the issue ought again to be discussed at ministerial level. In July 1963 the three nuclear powers signed a nuclear test ban treaty in Moscow.

▶ **SOURCE D** *British Prime Minister Wilson, 1968:*

We intend to make to the alliances of which we are a member a contribution related to our economic capability. While recognising that our security lies in Europe and must be based on NATO, we have accordingly decided to accelerate withdrawal of our forces from the stations in the Far East by the end of 1971 ... and from the Persian Gulf ... By that date we shall not be maintaining military bases outside Europe and the Mediterranean.

SECTION A: KU — GENERAL

1 In what ways was Britain weakened as an international power after 1945? (4)

2 For what reasons did Britain manage to maintain some prestige as a world power despite her weakened state? (4)

3 How important was military strength in determining a nation's international reputation and influence after 1945? Explain your answer. (4)

SECTION B: EV — GEN/CREDIT

1 How useful are Sources A and D as evidence of Britain's international position in the 1940s and 1960s? (4)

2 Compare British status and importance as a world power as shown in Sources C and D. (4)

3 Does Source C or Source D more accurately describe Britain's real position as an international power in the 1950s and 1960s? Explain. (4)

· UNIT 2 · CONTEXT C ·
International Cooperation & Conflict, 1930s–1960s
THREATS TO WORLD PEACE: BERLIN

The 'German Problem' reached a crisis point in 1948 when Stalin tried to seal off divided Berlin from the West.

▶ **SOURCE A** *Adapted from a memoir by US Secretary of State Averell Harriman:*

The blockade of Berlin concerned people very deeply ... General Clay (US Army Commander in Germany) wanted to force the tanks through. We had at that time still a monopoly in nuclear weapons and President Truman ... decided to go ahead with the airlift and Britain played a very important role in this.

▶ **SOURCE B** *British Labour Party politician Denis Healey:*

The problem was that those Americans who became interested in foreign affairs in the post-war period tended to see Communism as an absolute evil ... The Americans were easily persuaded by Soviet behaviour in Berlin and Czechoslovakia that the Russians were really out for world conquest.

▶ **SOURCE C** *From a secondary text:*

The Western Powers organised the 'Berlin Airlift' ... British and American planes, service and civilian, flew by night and day over many months to maintain supplies to the western sectors of the city ... In all over 250,000 flights were made.

▶ **SOURCE D** *From a secondary text:*

Three million people had escaped to the west between 1949 and 1961. During the night of 13 August units of the East German Army supported by Russian tanks closed all the crossings from East Berlin to the West. Trains were turned back, road traffic halted and workmen brought in to lay barbed wire and behind this to build, on land in the Soviet Sector, the Wall ... The East German leader claimed the Wall was to stop 'fascist infiltrators' crossing from the West. The majority of East Berliners accepted that there would be no easy way of getting to the West. The improvement in the East German economic performance may be dated from the building of the Wall.

▶ **SOURCE E** *US President J. F. Kennedy, 1963:*

All free men wherever they may be are citizens of Berlin, and thus I take pride in saying 'Ich bin ein Berliner' ('I am a Berliner').

SECTION A: KU — GENERAL

1 Describe Russian actions in Berlin between 1948 and 1961. (4)

2 For what reasons was the Russian blockade of Berlin a threat to world peace? (3)

3 How important was the building of the Berlin Wall to the development of international relations in the 1960s? Fully explain your answer. (5)

SECTION B: EV — GEN/CREDIT

1 How valuable is Source A as evidence of the attitudes of the USA towards Berlin? (3)

2 Do Sources A and B give similar or differing pictures of US and British attitudes towards Berlin? Explain your answer. (4)

3 Discuss the relevance of the sources in explaining Berlin's importance in international affairs in the post-1945 world. (5)

UNIT 2 · CONTEXT C ·
International Cooperation & Conflict, 1930s–1960s
SEARCH FOR SECURITY: UNO

▶**SOURCE A** *Extract from UN Charter, 1945. UNO aims:*

To save succeeding generations from the scourge of war which twice in our lifetime has brought untold suffering to mankind, and to reaffirm faith in fundamental human rights, in the dignity and worth of the human person, in the equal rights of men and women and of nations large and small.

Comments on UNO and world peace:

▶**SOURCE B** *A historian's comment:*

There was no issue on which the Super-powers did not find themselves involved ... almost invariably on opposite sides. The USA and other western powers regarded the Security Council veto merely as an ultimate safeguard ... the Soviet Union regarded it as an everyday weapon of diplomacy to prevent any decision of which she strongly disapproved.

▶**SOURCE C** *Denis Healey Autobiography:*

Soviet foreign policy after the war was based on the Leninist doctrine of the Two Camps. This held that the Communist and Capitalist worlds were condemned to a struggle which must end in the victory of one side or the other. It rejected in principle the concept of a world society on which the United Nations was based.

▶**SOURCE D** *Soviet Foreign Minister, 1947:*

The Truman Doctrine is a glowing example of the way in which the principles of the United Nations are ignored. The USA has moved towards giving up the idea of international cooperation and joint action by the great powers. It has tried to force its will on independent countries, using the money distributed as relief to needy countries as a means of putting political pressure on these countries.

▶**SOURCE E** *US Defence Minister, 1956:*

I do not care how many words are written into the UN Charter about not using force; if in fact there is not a substitute for force, and some way of getting just solutions of (world) problems, inevitably the world will fall back into anarchy and into chaos.

SECTION A: KU — GENERAL

1 Describe the aims of the United Nations Organisation and the means through which it tried to achieve these aims. (5)

2 Explain the weaknesses of UNO as an international peace-keeping agency. (3)

3 How serious were the USA and the USSR in supporting the aims and principles of UNO? Explain your answer. (4)

SECTION B: EV — GEN/CREDIT

1 How useful are Sources D and E as evidence of great power attitudes to UNO? (4)

2 Do Sources B, C and D show similarities in the great power attitudes towards UNO? Explain your answer. (4)

3 How significant are the sources in explaining the effectiveness of UNO as an international institution? (4)

UNIT 2 · CONTEXT C
International Cooperation & Conflict, 1930s–1960s
THREATS TO WORLD PEACE: CUBA 1962

In 1962 a crisis in US-Soviet relations was reached.

▶ **SOURCE A** *From a secondary text:*

In the most acute crisis of East–West rivalry Britain was little more than a spectator. In 1962 President Castro of Cuba allowed the Russians to begin installing nuclear missiles on the island — an action which would have rendered useless the warning system of the USA and put that country in mortal peril. US President Kennedy ordered a blockade of Cuba and demanded the withdrawal of the missiles.

▶ **SOURCE B** *President Kennedy, in a TV/radio broadcast, 22 October:*

This secret build-up of communist missiles is a provocative change in the *status quo* which cannot be accepted ... To halt this a strict quarantine on all military equipment under shipment to Cuba is being instituted ... This nation will regard any nuclear missile launched from Cuba against any nation in the western hemisphere as an attack by the Soviet Union on the USA, requiring a full retaliatory response upon the Soviet Union.

▶ **SOURCE C** *Map of Cuba and the USA.*

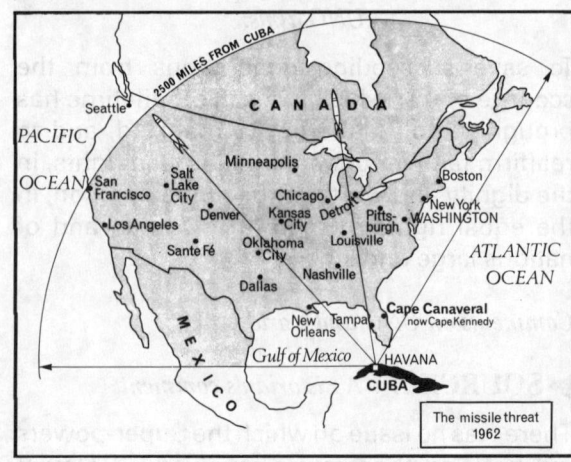

The missile threat 1962

▶ **SOURCE D** *Soviet leader Nikita Kruschev, in a personal memoir:*

I will explain what the Caribbean Crisis of 1962 was all about. We were quite sure the Americans would never reconcile themselves to the existence of Castro's Cuba ... They feared that a socialist Cuba might become a magnet that would attract other Latin American countries to socialism ... We had to establish an effective deterrent to US interference in the Caribbean. The logical answer was missiles ... I had the idea of installing nuclear missiles in Cuba without letting the USA find out until it was too late to do anything about them ... We had no desire to start a war ... We sent the Americans a note saying that we agreed to remove our missiles only if the President assured us there would be no invasion of Cuba ... Kennedy gave in. It was a great victory for us.

SECTION A: KU — GENERAL

1. In what ways was President Kennedy's response to the Cuban missile build-up a tough response? (4)

2. Why did the Crisis represent a serious danger to world peace? (4)

3. Was the outcome of the Crisis a victory for either the USA or the USSR? Explain your answer. (4)

SECTION B: EV — GEN/CREDIT

1. How useful is Source B as evidence of Kennedy's intentions with regard to the Cuban Crisis? (4)

2. Do Sources A and D give similar or differing accounts of the Crisis? Support your answer. (4)

3. How accurate is Kruschev's account of the Crisis as put forward in Source D? (4)

UNIT 2 · CONTEXT C ·
International Cooperation and Conflict, 1930s–1960s
CREDIT LEVEL — KU QUESTIONS

1 *On 30 September 1938 the decision was announced. Hitler was to have the whole of Sudetenland; he promised he had no other demands in Europe. That promise was short-lived.*

How important was lack of decisiveness from government leaders in Britain and elsewhere in encouraging Hitler's ambitions for German expansion in the late 1930s in Europe? (4)

2 *Total war involved all citizens, civilian as well as military.*

Choosing **either** Germany **or** Britain, describe the ways in which civilians were affected by the continuing war in Europe and elsewhere between 1939 and 1945. (8)
For this question you should write a short essay of several paragraphs.

3 *The Second World War was essentially the first major conflict in which superior technology played a vital part in securing victory.*

Discuss the importance of technology in determining the eventual outcome of the Second World War. (4)

4 *The aftermath of war in reality speeded up an already well-established decline in Britain's status as a world power.*

For what main reasons did Britain's status as a world power decline after 1945? (4)

5 *'I do not care how many fine words are written in the UN Charter about not using force. If there is not some way of getting just solutions to be enforced, the world will fall back into anarchy.'*
(US Defence Minister 1956)

To what extent was UNO's international role weakened by its reluctance to use force against international aggressors? (4)

6 *'Mr President there is hard photographic evidence that the Russians have offensive weapons in Cuba.'*
(US National Security Adviser, 16 October 1962)

Describe how the Cuban Missile Crisis developed and how it was finally resolved. (4)

UNIT 3 · CONTEXT A ·
People and Power: USA 1850–80
SLAVERY AND THE CIVIL WAR

▶ **SOURCE A** *From a secondary text:*

Most plantations worked the gang system ... whereby slave-drivers supervised teams of workers, male and female. The field slaves, like most free farmers, worked approximately twelve hours a day, six days a week during the growing season. In the off-season the work pace was relaxed.

But there was frequent use of the whip to maintain discipline and the risk of being sold away from friends and family.

A healthy, reasonably satisfied slave worked better than a sick one. So basic care of slaves, especially on large plantations, was good.

Their diet was ample with a high protein count. Medical care was adequate. Housing was cramped and clothing rough, but both were always provided ... There was time off and promotion to preferred jobs for good work.

▶ **SOURCE B** *A white Southerner's comment:*

Northerners have no idea of the depth of degradation — of poverty, hardship and humiliation — involved in that word slavery: if they had they would never cease in their efforts until so horrible a system was overthrown.

In 1859, John Brown, a Northern abolitionist, was executed by a Southern court for trying to spark a slave rebellion in Missouri.

▶ **SOURCE C** *Adapted from Brown's closing address at his trial:*

I see a book kissed here which I suppose to be the Bible ... That teaches me that whatsoever I would wish that men should do to me, I should so do even to them. It teaches me to 'remember them that are in bonds, as bound with them'. I endeavoured to act up to that instruction ... I believe that to have interfered as I have done — as I freely admitted I have done — on behalf of the despised poor was not wrong but right ... If it is deemed necessary that I should forfeit my life for the furtherance of the ends of justice, and mingle my blood further ... with the blood of millions in this slave country whose rights are disregarded by wicked, cruel and unjust laws, I submit, 'So let it be done.'

▶ **SOURCE D** *An abolitionist, writing in 1859:*

He is not 'Old Brown' any longer; he is an angel of light. I see now that it was necessary that the bravest and humanest man in all the country should be hung — I almost fear that I may yet hear of his deliverance, doubting if a prolonged life, if any life, can do as much good as his death.

SECTION A: KU — GENERAL

1 What were the effects of the plantation system as this existed in the Southern States of the USA? (4)

2 For what reasons did some people wish to change the plantation system? (4)

3 How important a figure was John Brown in the development of the slavery issue in the USA? (4)

SECTION B: EV — GEN/CREDIT

1 Are Sources C and D biased? Explain your answer. (4)

2 Do Sources A and B give a consistently similar view of slavery in the American South? Explain your answer. (4)

3 How typical were the views expressed in Source C in the USA in the 1850s? (4)

UNIT 3 · CONTEXT A ·
People and Power: USA 1850–80
ABRAHAM LINCOLN AND HIS IDEA OF THE UNION

During the 1850s, slavery became an urgent issue in the USA.

▶ **SOURCE A** *Adapted from a speech made by Senator Daniel Webster, 1850:*

I have heard that the idea has been considered that after the break up of the Union (of the USA), a Southern Confederacy might be formed.

The idea, so far as it exists, must be of a separation setting the slave states to one side and the free states to the other. I hold the idea of a separation of these states as an impossibility. We could not draw a line of separation that would satisfy any five men in the country.

▶ **SOURCE B** *Adapted from a speech made by Abraham Lincoln in 1858:*

I believe that this government (of the USA) cannot endure permanently half-slave and half-free ... Either the opponents of slavery will arrest the further spread of it ... or its advocates will push it forward till it shall become alike lawful in all the states — North as well as South ... I do not expect the Union to be dissolved ... I do not expect the house to fall — but I do expect it will cease to be divided. It will become all one thing or all the other.

▶ **SOURCE C** *Adapted from a secondary text:*

Why did the cotton states act so precipitately? Their haste in severing the bonds of union reflected a hatred of the Yankee that had been growing for decades. The Yankee devil had been blamed for every Southern difficulty. If manufactured goods were expensive, it was because of the Yankee tariff. If cotton growers made no profit it was because of the Yankee middle-man. The conviction had grown that the South had lost more than it gained from the Federal Union. 'Then why', demanded the Charleston Mercury, 'should we any longer submit to the yoke of our tyrant brother the domineering, abolitionist North!'

▶ **SOURCE D** *Lincoln, in his Second Inaugural Address, 1865:*

Both parties deprecated war, but one of them would make war rather than let the nation survive, and the other would accept war rather than let it perish. And the war came.

SECTION A: KU — GENERAL

1 Describe the growing conflict over the slavery issue in the USA in the 1850s. (4)

2 Explain how conflict over slavery and other issues led to civil war in the USA. (4)

3 Was the North or the South more responsible for bringing about civil war? Explain. (4)

SECTION B: EV — GEN/CREDIT

1 How valuable is Source A in explaining the underlying causes of civil war in the USA? (4)

2 Do Sources A and B give similar or differing views of the North–South conflict in the USA? Explain your answer. (4)

3 To what extent do the sources give significant evidence on the career of Abraham Lincoln? (4)

UNIT 3 · CONTEXT A
People and Power: USA 1850–80
WESTWARD EXPANSION

Westward expansion in the 1850s

▶ **SOURCE A** *A wagon train going west — preparing for nightfall.*

▶ **SOURCE B** *'Fools of the Forty-Nine':*

The people died on every route,
They sickened and died like sheep.
And those at sea before they were dead,
Were launched into the deep.
And those that died crossing the plains,
Fared not as well as that,
For a hole was dug and they was dumped,
Along the terrible Platte.

▶ **SOURCE C** *From a secondary text:*

1852 was the biggest year of all in the goldfields for 81 million dollars worth of gold was mined while the population of California had shot up to a quarter of a million. By 1900 more than 1,000 million dollars worth of gold had been found.

Westward expansion in the 1870s

▶ **SOURCE D** *From a secondary text:*

To make their lines pay, the railway companies had to encourage hundreds of thousands of settlers to live on the prairie lands. Huge advertising campaigns were undertaken by them in the East and in Europe. Largely due to their efforts the prairies were settled and developed. ... The railways sustained the settlers once they were there. The railways carried food, clothing, furniture and timber for barns and houses ... New seeds and tools were also carried; steel ploughs, barbed wire, drills, windmills, mechanical reapers and binders and steam traction engines.

▶ **SOURCE E** *Eye-witness, Omaha station, 1880s:*

'Lunches put up for people going west'. This sign was on the corner. Passengers were eating hastily — they knew it would be long before they ate again. Provident Germans bought sausage by the yard, babies got bits of it to keep them quiet. Murderous looking rifles and guns, with strapped rolls of worn and muddy blankets stood here and there; murderous but jolly-looking miners strode about, keeping an eye on their weapons and bedding. Well-dressed women and men with polished shoes lounged up and down, curious and amused.

SECTION A: KU — GENERAL

1 What dangers faced the early settlers during their journey westward? (3)

2 For what reasons were settlers persuaded to move west? Fully explain your answer. (5)

3 How important were railroads in the development of the American west? Explain. (4)

SECTION B: EV — GEN/CREDIT

1 How reliable are Sources A and B as evidence of the westward journeys of the settlers? (4)

2 Compare the descriptions of experiences of western settlers in the 1850s and 1870s as given in Sources A, B and E. (4)

3 Do the sources accurately show the changing face of the west during the period between 1850 and 1880? Explain. (4)

· UNIT 3 · CONTEXT A ·
People and Power: USA 1850–80
INDIAN OPPOSITION TO WESTWARD EXPANSION

In the 1860s the first Sioux revolt took place.

▶ **SOURCE A** *Fort Kearney, which was destroyed by a Sioux war party in 1868.*

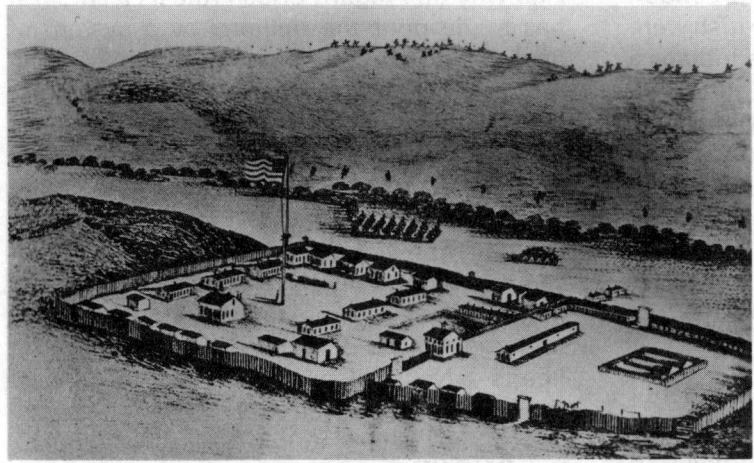

▶ **SOURCE B** *From a secondary text:*

Red Cloud's War was triggered off when the whites decided to protect the Bozeman Trail, which ran from Wyoming to the goldfields of Montana, by building a road and a series of forts. The Sioux leader Red Cloud was willing to talk. Just as it looked as if he might sign ... into Fort Laramie rode Col. Carrington and 700 officers and men. Furiously Red Cloud rose and said: 'The Great White Father sends us presents and wants us to sell him the road, but before the Indians say yes or no, White Chief goes with soldiers to steal the road.'

In the mid 1870s the 'Sioux War' began.

▶ **SOURCE C** *From a secondary text:*

In 1868 Custer attacked a Cheyenne camp ... Chief Kettle died along with many women and children. Custer found plenty of evidence of gold in the Black Hills and broadcast the news on his return. The result was a stampede, with the Government powerless to keep the prospectors out. An offer of cash was made to the Indians for the Black Hills. Red Cloud, now 'tame', was willing to negotiate, but younger men like Sitting Bull, Crazy Horse and Gall were not ... In the bitter winter of 1875, those Sioux who had left their reservations because they did not feel bound by treaties they had not signed, were ordered to return to them. Most of them refused and the following year a three-pronged invasion of Indian country was launched.

▶ **SOURCE D** *Sioux Ghost Dance:*

Father help us.
Take away the white man,
Send back the buffalo.
We are poor and weak ...
Help us to be what we once were:
Happy hunters of buffalo.

▶ **SOURCE E** *White friend of the Indians:*

The Red man was the true American. The history of how they fought for their country is written in blood, a stain that time cannot grind out. Their God was the sun, their church all outdoors.

SECTION A: KU — GENERAL

1 How did the government of the USA try to win control of Indian lands in the west? (4)

2 Were the causes of Red Cloud's War and of the 1876 Sioux War similar? Explain your answer. (4)

3 Was war between the White and Indian Americans inevitable? Explain your answer. (4)

SECTION B: EV — GEN/CREDIT

1 How useful are Sources D and E as evidence of beliefs and attitudes of American Indians? (4)

2 To what extent do Sources A, B and C give similar views of White American treatment of the American Indians? Explain your answer. (4)

3 Was the view of American Indians put forward in Source E common among American Whites? Explain. (4)

UNIT 3 · CONTEXT B ·
People and Power: India 1917-47
DISCONTENT AGAINST BRITISH RULE IN INDIA

▶ **SOURCE A** *From a secondary text:*

In 1917 India had been promised 'Responsible government' but no transfer of power. The viceroy still ruled, the India Office in London still wielded final authority. Yet the British were digging their own graves. They gave Indians a European education, and with this education came the demand for national independence. The Indian National Congress had long called for this in a modest way. It now found an inspired leader in Gandhi, barrister, saint and wily politician.

▶ **SOURCE B** *From a secondary text:*

Amid a good deal of unrest in 1919 the episode at Amritsar stood out. Following the murder of four Europeans by a mob, an unarmed crowd assembled in an enclosed garden. It failed to disperse when ordered to do so: whereupon General Dyer ordered his soldiers to fire upon it. Firing continued for ten minutes. Bullets and panic took the lives of 379 and 1208 persons were wounded. The Amritsar massacre was not soon forgotten, the more so because Dyer received much support in debates in the British Parliament in July 1920. Against this background Mahatma Gandhi and the Congress Party launched the campaign for India's independence.

Two views of British rule in India

▶ **SOURCE C** *Gandhi:*

And why do I regard British rule as a curse? It has made poor the millions by a system of exploitation and by a ruinous expensive military and civil government which the country can never afford. It has reduced us to political slavery. The British system seems designed to crush the very life out of the peasant ... My ambition is: to convert the British people through non-violence, and then make them see the wrong they have done to India. If the Indian people join me, the sufferings they will undergo will be enough to melt the stoniest hearts. Non-violence will be organised through civil disobedience.

▶ **SOURCE D** *A British civil servant in India, from a contemporary novel:*

'We're out here to do justice and keep the peace.'
'Your sentiments are those of a god.' ...
'There's no point in all this. Here we are and we're going to stay. And the country's got to put up with us, gods or no gods!'

SECTION A: KU — GENERAL

1 Describe British attitudes towards India during the period 1917 to 1920. (3)

2 Explain the causes of Indian discontent against the British in India. (4)

3 How important was Gandhi in the developing conflict over British rule in India? Fully explain your answer. (5)

SECTION B: EV — GEN/CREDIT

1 How valuable is Source C as evidence of Indian attitudes towards British rule in India? (4)

2 In what ways do Sources A and B appear to support the view of British rule put forward in Source C? (4)

3 Do you believe that the views put forward in Source D were typical of British administrators in India? Explain your answer. (4)

UNIT 3 · CONTEXT B ·
People and Power: India 1917-47
INDIAN INDEPENDENCE AND PARTITION

▶ **SOURCE A** *India and Pakistan 1947-50.*

▶ **SOURCE B** *Adapted from a secondary text:*

Attlee was convinced that Britain must leave India, but must do so in the manner least disruptive to India and least harmful to Britain. Separation (of Hindu and Moslem areas in India) had to be arranged ... Mr Jinnah and the Moslem League had gained in strength. Attlee sent out Lord Mountbatten as Viceroy ... to end the British Raj. By force of personality he got Gandhi, Nehru and Jinnah all discussing together how to take over power without chaos: and Attlee announced in February 1947 that whatever happened, Britain would leave India not later than 1 June 1948.

▶ **SOURCE C** *Adapted from the memoirs of British Prime Minister Attlee:*

It was useless to try to get agreement by discussion between the leaders of the rival communities. Unless these men were faced with the urgency of a time limit, there would always be delay. As long as Britain held power it was always possible to attribute failure to her. India must be faced with the fact that in a short space of time it would have responsibility thrust upon it ... The new viceroy ... soon showed his quality. Indian leaders were constantly reminded that the sands were running out. Hindus and Moslems however found it impossible to agree on a single government for the whole of India ... and it was by the decision of the Indians themselves that a partition was made.

▶ **SOURCE D** *From a secondary text:*

On 15 August 1947, two Dominions, India and Pakistan, the latter in two parts, were instituted. Riots and considerable bloodshed ensued. grave loss of life, as well as partition, was the price of independence. But the Indian Independence Act opened a new era in the long story of Anglo-Indian relations. Some 400 million people — one-sixth of all humanity — gained political independence overnight. That they were capable of receiving it was due to the progressive measures of semi-independence granted since 1919.

SECTION A: KU — GENERAL

1 Describe Prime Minister Attlee's plan for creating an independent India. (4)

2 Why was the establishment of independence in India accompanied by violence and loss of life? (4)

3 Was as much as possible done to limit the disruption brought about by the move to independence in India in 1947-48? Explain. (4)

SECTION B: EV — GEN/CREDIT

1 How useful is Source C as evidence of British policy towards India? (4)

2 To what extent does Source B support the evidence put forward in Source C? (4)

3 Do the sources accurately and fully describe the problems involved in bringing about Indian independence? Support your answer. (4)

UNIT 3 · CONTEXT C
People and Power: Russia 1914–41
DISCONTENT UNDER THE TSAR

▶ SOURCE A *An anti-Tsarist war poster.*

The slogan reads 'Help for the starving'

▶ SOURCE B *Adapted from a secondary text:*

Russian losses averaged 300,000 a month. Troops were put into the front lines without arms. They fought with clubs until the death of a comrade freed a rifle. Artillery reserves were exhausted by November 1914. The transport system fell apart. Despite conscription of peasants ... women, children and older men managed to plant and harvest large crops ... But these could not be moved to the cities and only with enormous effort was the army kept fed. The cities began to feel the pinch while huge stocks built up in the countryside. In Siberia butter sold for a few kopeks a kilo, in Moscow it could hardly be bought.

▶ SOURCE C *From a Russian historical novel:*

Some of the regiments lost half of their complement of men and horses. Four hundred Cossacks and sixteen officers were killed and wounded in Listnitsky's regiment alone. 'We may lose a few hundred thousand soldiers, but it is the duty of everyone this country has nurtured to defend the fatherland from enslavement.' Listnitsky puffed at his cigarette and removed his pince-nez to clean his glasses, staring the while at Bunchuk with his short-sighted eyes. 'The workers have no fatherland,' Bunchuk stamped the words out. 'There is the deepest truth in these words of Marx. We never have had, and we still have no fatherland. This accursed country gave you your food and drink, but we workers grow like wormwood on the steppe ... We and you can't flourish together.'

▶ SOURCE D *Lenin, in a pamphlet published in 1916:*

The tens of millions of dead and maimed left by the war open the eyes of the tens of millions who are downtrodden, oppressed, and duped by the bourgeoisie ... Thus out of universal ruin caused by war, a world-wide revolutionary crisis is arising which ... cannot end in any other way than in a proletarian revolution and its victory.

SECTION A: KU — GENERAL

1 What problems were faced by people living in Russia during the First World War? (4)

2 To what extent were problems within wartime Russia caused by poor government? (4)

3 How important were the effects of war in bringing about a revolutionary situation within Russia by 1917? Explain your answer. (4)

SECTION B: EV — GEN/CREDIT

1 How reliable are Sources A and D as evidence of the effects of war on the Russian people? (5)

2 Do Sources C and D provide similar or differing views on the effects of war within Russia? Explain your answer. (3)

3 Were the views put forward in Source D shared by many Russians in 1916? Support your answer. (4)

UNIT 3 · CONTEXT C ·
People and Power: Russia 1914–41
DISCONTENT UNDER THE TSAR / FEBRUARY REVOLUTION

Causes of discontent in Russia

▶ **SOURCE A** *Rodzianko (Duma President), March 1917:*

The disturbances which have begun in Petrograd are becoming more serious... Shortages of bread and flour cause panic. There is complete distrust of the government... The defence plants in Petrograd have ceased work because of lack of fuel and raw materials. The workers are without jobs, the unemployed take the path to riot and revolt.

Two telegrams to Tsar Nicholas on the Petrograd disturbances

▶ **SOURCE B** *From Tsarina Alexandra, 10 March:*

This is a hooligan movement, young people run and shout that there is no bread, simply to create excitement, along with workers who prevent others from working. If the weather was very cold they would all probably stay at home. But all this will pass and become calm if only the Duma will behave itself.

▶ **SOURCE C** *From Rodzianko, 11 March:*

The capital is in a state of anarchy. The Government is paralysed; the transport system is broken down. The food and fuel suppliers are completely disorganised... There is wild shooting on the streets; troops are firing at each other. It is urgent that someone the people trust is allowed to set up a new government. There must be no delay.

▶ **SOURCE D** *From a historical memoir by Alexander Kerensky:*

By sunset, March 13th, all Petrograd was already in the hands of the revolutionary troops. The old Government had ceased to function. Some of the Government buildings were already occupied by the revolutionaries, others, such as the offices of the secret police, the law courts, were on fire. In the Duma we had created a central authority to control the troops and head the revolt.

▶ **SOURCE E** *The Tsar's abdication note, 15 March:*

The internal disturbances... threaten to have a calamitous effect on the further conduct of a hard-fought war... The war must be carried to a victorious conclusion... In these decisive days we have deemed it our duty to help our people draw closer together and, in agreement with the Duma, we have judged it right to abdicate the throne.

SECTION A: KU — GENERAL

1. What were the main problems facing the Russian government in March 1917? (4)

2. Why did Tsar Nicholas fail to deal effectively with growing unrest in Petrograd? (4)

3. How important were the policies and actions of the Russian Duma in bringing about the downfall of Tsarism? Explain. (4)

SECTION B: EV — GEN/CREDIT

1. How useful are Sources A and C as evidence of the situation in Petrograd in March 1917? (4)

2. Why do Sources B and C give such differing accounts of the situation in Petrograd? (4)

3. Does Source D give an honest and accurate explanation of the Tsar's reasons for abdication? Explain your answer. (4)

UNIT 3 · CONTEXT C
People and Power: Russia 1914–41
DISCONTENT UNDER PROVISIONAL GOVERNMENT

The provisional government and the continuing war

▶ **SOURCE A** *Bolshevik parade, 1917.*

▶ **SOURCE B** *A typical soldier's response (recorded by John Reed, Bolshevik sympathiser, Autumn 1917):*

Show me what we are fighting for, is it the democracy or is it the capitalist plunderers? If you can prove to me that I am defending the Revolution then I'll go out and fight without capital punishment to force me! When the land belongs to the peasants, and the factories to the workers and the power to the Soviets, then we'll know we have something to fight for, and we'll fight for it!

▶ **SOURCE C** *From a secondary text:*

With the slogan 'Peace! Bread! Land!', the Bolsheviks could show themselves the only party campaigning for the things most wanted by the masses. If new elections took place for union leaders, army committees and the Soviets, it would be Bolsheviks who were elected in place of Mensheviks and SRs. At the same time 'Peace! Bread! Land!' would weaken the government's position. With a weak government and Soviets controlled by the Bolsheviks, it would be time, Lenin said, to bring into play his second slogan, 'All Power to the Soviets.'

▶ **SOURCE D** *Adapted from a statement made by Kerensky:*

The measures proposed by the Provisional Government were revolutionary for they envisaged the total transfer of the land to those who worked on it . . . This decision enraged the landowners who tried to thwart it . . . On Lenin's instructions the Bolsheviks incited the most backward elements in the countryside to take the law into their own hands . . . Critics were later to write that the Provisional Government had been 'too slow' with the land reform. But they failed to explain how it could have been carried out any more quickly over the whole expanse of Russia at the height of a terrible war.

SECTION A: KU — GENERAL

1 What were the main complaints made against the Provisional Government? (4)

2 Why was the Provisional Government generally unsuccessful in dealing with the major problems facing Russia in 1917? (5)

3 Was discontent in rural or in urban areas of Russia the most important reason for growing popularity of the Bolsheviks? Explain. (3)

SECTION B: EV — GEN/CREDIT

1 How useful are Sources A and B as evidence of people's attitudes towards the Bolsheviks in the autumn of 1917 in Russia? (4)

2 Do Sources B and C give consistently similar views on solutions to Russia's problems in 1917? (4)

3 Do Sources C and D accurately explain Lenin's rise and Kerensky's fall in popularity? Explain your answer. (4)

UNIT 3 · CONTEXT C ·
People and Power: Russia 1914–41
OCTOBER REVOLUTION, 1917

Lenin and the need for an armed takeover of power, October 1917

▶**SOURCE A** *From a secondary history text:*

Lenin offered his resignation from the Bolshevik Central Committee to regain his freedom to talk with the ordinary members of the party: 'For it is my profound conviction that if we wait for the Congress of Soviets and let slip the present moment, we shall ruin the revolution' ... On October 23rd Lenin came in disguise to Petrograd ... His presence was enough to tip the scale. By a majority of ten votes to two the Committee decided to prepare for armed insurrection ... Six days later the Petrograd Soviet created a Military Revolutionary Committee under Trotsky as President of the Soviet. This body made the military preparations for the revolution.

Beginning of the Bolshevik takeover (7 November)

▶**SOURCE B** *Bolshevik eye-witness account:*

The decisive operation of the military revolutionary committee started around two in the morning ... No resistance was shown ... The stations, bridges, telegraphs and telegraphic agency were occupied by small forces brought from the barracks. Military operations in the politically important city centres resembled a changing of the guard ... not one casualty was recorded. The city was absolutely calm.

▶**SOURCE C** *From the historical memoir of Leon Trotsky:*

At 2.35 in the afternoon (of 7 November 1917), an emergency session of the Petrograd Soviet opened with a report from Trotsky who in the name of the Military Revolutionary Committee announced that the Provisional Government no longer existed ... 'They told us that an insurrection would drown the revolution in torrents of blood ... We do not know of a single casualty' ... Lenin, who appeared publicly for the first time after emerging from underground, briefly outlined the programme of the Revolution: to break up the old government apparatus; to create a new system of government through the Soviets; to take measures for immediate cessation of war; to abolish the landlords' property rights; to establish workers' control over production. 'The third Russian Revolution', he said, 'must in the end lead to the victory of socialism.'

▶**SOURCE D** *Trotsky, speaking to other parties in Petrograd Soviet:*

An uprising of the people needs no justification. We have been strengthening the revolutionary energy of the workers and soldiers. Our uprising has won. And now we are being asked to give up our victory — to come to an agreement with SRs and Mensheviks — with wretched disunited individuals. You are bankrupt! Your past is over. Go to the place where you belong from now on — the dust-bin of history!

SECTION A: KU — GENERAL

1 Describe the preparations made for the Bolshevik rising of November 1917. (4)

2 Explain the effects of the Bolshevik takeover for Russia as a whole. (3)

3 How important was the contribution of Leon Trotsky in achieving power for the Bolshevik party in Russia? Fully explain your answer. (5)

SECTION B: EV — GEN/CREDIT

1 How useful is Source B as evidence of the events of 7 November 1917 in Petrograd? (4)

2 Does Source B support the account of the rising given in Source C? Explain your answer. (3)

3 Do the sources taken together provide a full and accurate account of the events of October–November 1917 in Russia? Fully explain. (5)

UNIT 3 · CONTEXT C
People and Power: Russia 1914–41
CIVIL WAR — WAR COMMUNISM

▶ **SOURCE A** *A Bolshevik poster.*

The figures represent a French army general, a capitalist-businessman, a Tsarist army general, SR leader Chernov.

There was an attempt on Lenin's life in September 1918.

▶ **SOURCE B** *Adapted from the Bolshevik Party Report, 1918:*

Each drop of Lenin's blood must be paid for in hundreds of deaths. The interests of the Revolution demand extermination of the bourgeoisie.... An end to this mercy! All SRs to be arrested by local Soviets. Mass shootings to be the rule!

▶ **SOURCE C** *Cheka Chief Dzerzhinsky, 1918:*

The Cheka is not a Court. The Cheka is the defence of the Revolution. As in the Civil War the Red Army cannot stop to ask whether it may harm particular individuals ... so the Cheka must defend the Revolution even if its sword falls occasionally on the heads of the innocent.

▶ **SOURCE D** *Adapted from a secondary text:*

(By 1921) Russian industry had almost completely collapsed. Half the workers disappeared; they had either died from fighting, starvation, disease or had gone home to the villages in the hope of finding food ... people blamed the government and communism. Peasants held that the cause of their hardship was the requisitioning bands; in many cases they refused to plant crops except to provide food for their own needs ... Trade unionists complained of the system of workers' books and the muddling of the planners in Moscow whom they blamed for the collapse of industry ... Control over the management of industries should be given to the unions and taken from the Communist Party. Then in 1921 the Kronstadt sailors ... rose against the Communist government they had helped to put into power.

SECTION A: KU — GENERAL

1 Describe fully the problems faced by the new Bolshevik government between 1918 and 1921. (5)

2 Explain why discontent was widespread among the Russian people by 1921. (4)

3 To what extent did the Bolshevik government rule by deliberate use of terror in Russia? (3)

SECTION B: EV — GEN/CREDIT

1 What examples of bias and exaggeration can be seen in Source A? What is the purpose of these? (4)

2 Do Sources B and C provide similar and consistent evidence of Bolshevik attitudes in 1918? Support your answer. (4)

3 Were the views expressed in Sources B and C typical of Bolshevik viewpoints in 1918? Explain your answer. (4)

UNIT 3 · CONTEXT C
People and Power: Russia 1914–41
ACTIVITIES OF COMMUNIST GOVERMENT UNDER STALIN

Two extracts from writings and speeches of Stalin

▶ **SOURCE A** *(1927):*

Our country should not become a part of the capitalist system of world economy. The working and peasant classes and the leadership of the working class, should be strengthened and ... the conditions of the working class and of the rural poor should be steadily improved.

▶ **SOURCE B** *(1929):*

An offensive against the Kulaks is a serious matter. We must smash the Kulaks, eliminate them as a class ... We must strike so hard as to prevent them from rising to their feet again.

▶ **SOURCE C** *Comment of a British visitor in Stalin's Russia:*

The Soviets have not even the power to criticise that the Dumas had ... The national religion is becoming Stalinism. The peasants enjoy as little freedom as they did under the Tsar ... They are not only poor, they fear becoming rich in case they are branded as 'Kulaks'.

▶ **SOURCE D** *Comment by a Russian opponent of Stalinism in 1930:*

The Party is dominated by the Secretariat and the GPU which appreciates only the communist who obeys the Party's orders without question ... All the best socialists, who have devoted all their lives to the cause have been driven to suicide, jailed or exiled, and their characters defamed. The GPU ... has many of the ablest and most unscrupulous members of the old Tsarist Okrhana ... No trick is too mean for these people. It is even rumoured that two GPU chiefs and many others 'died suddenly' just when it suited Stalin that they should die.

▶ **SOURCE E** *A description of Stalinist show trials and purges, taken from a secondary text:*

The usual tactic was to produce signed 'confessions' in court, whereby the prisoner repented of crimes against the State which he never had committed. Such confessions were obtained by various means including physical and mental torture. The purges of the Communist party began in 1934 and as these continued throughout the mid-thirties, some 500,000 party members were executed or sent to the labour camps. The body responsible for carrying out the purges was the NKVD, set up in 1934. The NKVD took in the GPU, the secret police which had replaced the Cheka in the 1920s.

SECTION A: KU — GENERAL

1 Describe Stalin's policy aims in the period between 1927 and 1930. (4)

2 Why did Stalin wish to enforce and extend government control in Russia during this period? (4)

3 Was Stalinism or Communism the more important government ideology in Russia in the 1930s? Explain your answer. (4)

SECTION B: EV — GEN/CREDIT

1 How useful are Sources A, B and C as evidence of the effects of Stalin's policies in Russia? (4)

2 Do Sources D and E give similar or differing pictures of Stalinism in the 1930s? Explain your answer. (4)

3 Are the criticisms of Stalin made in Source D justifiable and accurate? Explain your answer. (4)

UNIT 3 · CONTEXT C
People and Power: Russia 1914–41
STALIN'S FIVE-YEAR PLANS

Russian propaganda posters, early 1930s

▶ **SOURCE A** *Sabotage by Kulaks.*

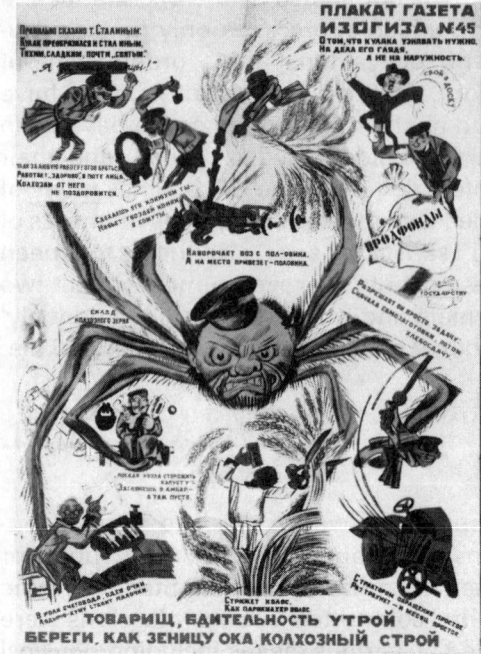

▶ **SOURCE B** *Enemies of the Five-Year Plans.*

▶ **SOURCE C** *From a secondary text:*

The emphasis was on state planning and the development of industry. Russia moved into the era of Stalin's Five-Year Plans when the shops were emptied of consumer goods because all efforts were concentrated on heavy industry. A new policy of collectivisation in agriculture was begun, whereby the creation of huge state farms drove peasants from the land into the factories ... The new policy was also designed to smash the wealthy middle-class peasant, the Kulak, who had benefited from NEP.

Results and effects of the Five-Year Plans, 1928–40

▶ **SOURCE D** *Russian output (million tons).*

	1928	1940
Steel	4.3	18.3
Coal	35.5	166.0
Oil	11.7	31.0
Cement	1.8	5.8
Grain	73.0	95.5
Tractors (actual figures)	1,200	31,000

▶ **SOURCE E** *Comments on the Five-Year Plans:*

'The factory owners under the NEP did not force us to work in four shifts and there was enough of everything in the shops ... Now we work in four shifts ... and the shops are empty.' (*Russian factory worker*)

'I'm an old Bolshevik. I worked in the underground against the Tsar and fought in the Civil War. Did I do all that in order that I should now surround villages with machine-guns and order my men to fire indiscriminately at peasants?' (*GPU officer enforcing collectivisation*)

SECTION A: KU — GENERAL

1 Fully describe the aims and achievements of Stalin's Five-Year Plans in the 1930s and 1940s. (5)

2 Why was there considerable opposition to the Five-Year Plans within Russia? (4)

3 How important were the Five-Year Plans for the development of Communism in Russia? (3)

SECTION B: EV — GEN/CREDIT

1 How reliable are Sources A and B as evidence about opposition to Stalin's government in the early 1930s? (4)

2 Do Sources C and E give similar or differing views on the Five-Year Plans? Support your answer. (4)

3 Do you think that the views expressed in Source E were typical of popular opinion in Russia in the 1930s and 1940s? Explain your answer. (4)

UNIT 3 · CONTEXT C
People and Power: Russia 1914–41
CREDIT QUESTIONS: KU

1 *'Out of universal ruin caused by war a revolutionary crisis is arising'.* (Lenin in 1917)

To what extent was the First World War responsible for the revolutionary situation in Russia by 1917? (4)

2 *Kerensky became the outstanding figure in the Provisional Government. No one swam in the rushing waters of the early revolution as did Kerensky. Not even Lenin.*

Fully discuss the importance of the role played by **either** Kerensky **or** Lenin in developments in Russia between March and November 1917. (8)
For this question you should write a short essay of several paragraphs.

3 *'To the Citizens of Russia: The Provisional Government is overthrown, State power is in the hands of the Petrograd Soviet'* (Public notice, 8 November 1917 in Petrograd)

Describe how power changed hands during the November Revolution in Russia. (4)

4 *'Our Party is for civil war. The civil war rages around the question of bread. We, the Soviets are on the offensive.'* (Leon Trotsky, June 1918)

Why did civil war come about in Russia between 1918 and 1922? (4)

5 *The basic ideas of Lenin's New Economic Policy were attacked by many, including Trotsky, who argued in favour of increasing War Communism.*

Describe the economic policies introduced by Lenin between 1918 and 1922. (4)

6 *In 1928, Stalin's First Five-Year Plan put the emphasis clearly on state economic planning. The economy was to be changed entirely with little regard for human costs or casualties.*

What were the effects of Stalin's Five-Year Plans on the Russian economy by 1940? (4)

7 *The Party was dominated by the Secretariat under Stalin's direction, and controlled by Stalin's State Police the GPU, which had many of the most unscrupulous members of the old Tsarist secret police.*

For what reasons did Stalin exercise control over the Communist party and, increasingly, over the ordinary citizens of Russia? Explain your answer fully. (4)

UNIT 3 · CONTEXT D ·
People and Power: Germany 1918–39
EFFECTS OF ENDING OF WAR IN GERMANY

▶ **SOURCE A** *Cartoon of the Kaiser (on right).*

▶ **SOURCE B** *From a secondary text:*

The Kaiser, in Berlin throughout October 1918, took a decision at the end of the month that was typical of the man... He ran away... He chose Hindenberg's Military Headquarters as a refuge. At Spa he was surrounded by generals including Groener, Ludendorff's successor, who were at first rigidly opposed to abdication ... As news from the warfront grew more desperate, the Kaiser declared himself ready to abdicate as German Emperor, but remain King of Prussia to lead the German troops back into the Fatherland. But the generals, more clearly aware of the mood and morale of the troops, told William, through Groener, that the troops would no longer follow him.

▶ **SOURCE C** *Two statements by P. Scheidemann, Deputy Leader, German SPD:*

(*In 1917*) This world war appears to us only as the mighty prelude to a still mightier event, to spiritual and social revolution such as the world has never experienced.

(*9 November 1918*) We have won all along the line; what is old no longer exists. Ebert has been appointed Chancellor... The task is now to consolidate our victory... The Hohenzollerns have abdicated. Take care that this proud day be not besmirched by anything. It will always be a day of honour in the history of Germany. Long live the German Republic!

▶ **SOURCE D** *From a secondary text:*

On the night of 9 November, a few hours after the Republic had been declared a telephone rang in the study of Ebert... Then and there the SPD Leader and the second-in-command of the German Army made a (secret) pact which was to determine the nation's fate. Ebert agreed to put down anarchy and Bolshevism and maintain the Army in all its tradition. Groener thereupon pledged the support of the Army in helping the new Government to establish itself.

SECTION A: KU — GENERAL

1 In what ways was the government set up in 1918 in Germany different from that which it replaced? (4)

2 Why did the Kaiser abdicate in November 1918? (4)

3 What was the importance of the German Army in influencing developments in Germany in November 1919? Explain your answer. (4)

SECTION B: EV — GEN/CREDIT

1 How useful is Source C as evidence about the changes brought about in 1917–18 in Germany? (4)

2 Do Sources A and B give similar views of the personality and character of the Kaiser? Explain your answer. (4)

3 Do Sources C and D accurately explain the part played by Ebert in establishing republican government in Germany? Explain your answer. (4)

UNIT 3 · CONTEXT D
People and Power: Germany 1918–39
THE WEIMAR REPUBLIC AND PEACE

▶ **SOURCE A** *From a secondary text:*

In mid-June the Germans were faced with an ultimatum. They must sign the (Versailles) Treaty or the war would be renewed. There was bitter debate in the German National Assembly which was meeting at Weimar. President Ebert called Hindenburg by telephone. Hindenburg said to Groener, his assistant, 'You know what the answer must be. I am going for a walk.' When the telephone rang again Groener replied: 'The Army could hold its own against the Poles in the east. It could not resist an Allied advance in the west.' This answer determined the majority of the Assembly to accept the Treaty.

▶ **SOURCE B** *Adapted from recollections of Hindenburg, reflecting on the 'humiliation' of the Versailles Treaty:*

In spite of the superiority of the enemy in men and material, we could have brought the struggle to a favourable result if unanimous co-operation had existed between the army and the government....

▶ **SOURCE C** *German newspaper headline on the signing of the Treaty.*

Vengeance! German Nation

Today in the Hall of Mirrors, the disgraceful Treaty is being signed. Do not forget it. The German people will with unceasing labour press forward to reconquer the place among nations to which it is entitled. Then will come vengeance for the shame of 1919.

▶ **SOURCE D** *Adapted from a secondary text:*

Many Germans blamed Government leaders for signing the Versailles Treaty. By the Treaty much land had been taken from Germany.... Germans were forced to agree to pay for all the damage caused by the war ... Even Germans who were glad the war was over felt this treatment was unfair ... Other Germans were more bitter ... They said the war had been lost because of plots by Jews and Socialists. They thought the Weimar Republic was too soft with such people. They had also been alarmed when German Communists had started a revolution just after the war. This revolt had been crushed, but every week there were riots ... in the streets of German towns. Between 1918 and 1922, 376 people were murdered in quarrels over politics.

▶ **SOURCE E** *Hitler in a speech of 1920:*

We need some national pride again. But who can we be proud of these days? Of Ebert perhaps! Of the government! We need a national will. We must not always say 'We can't do that'. We must be able to do it. In order to smash this disgraceful peace treaty, we must regard every means as justified. First there must be a nationalist mood and then will come the economic prosperity of the nation. We must have faith in our future!

SECTION A: KU — GENERAL

1 What aspects of the Versailles Treaty most displeased the German government and people? (4)

2 Why did the German government agree to sign the Versailles Treaty? (3)

3 How important were the issues raised by the Versailles Treaty in the politics of Germany in the first years of the Weimar Republic? Fully explain your answer. (5)

SECTION B: EV — GEN/CREDIT

1 How useful are Sources A and B as evidence about the signing of the Versailles Treaty? (4)

2 Do Sources C and E give similar views on the Versailles Treaty? Support your answer. (3)

3 Do Sources B, C and E give an accurate account of the views of the German people on the Versailles Treaty? Fully explain your answer. (5)

UNIT 3 · CONTEXT D ·
People and Power: Germany 1918–39
CHARACTERISTICS OF WEIMAR: OPPOSITION

▶ **SOURCE A** *From a secondary text:*

'Political power stems from the people,' the Weimar Constitution stated. Election to the Reichstag and State Parliaments was to be by universal suffrage, all over the age of twenty being able to vote. The individual was given full democratic freedom. 'All Germans are equal in the eyes of the law.' 'Personal liberty cannot be taken away.' 'Every German has the right to express his opinion freely.' A French professor, sympathetic to the ideals of the Constitution, stated, 'Germany is as strongly democratic as possible. The power of decision rests with the majority. But there are strong minorities to the right and to the left that would prefer a dictatorship.'

▶ **SOURCE B** *A Nazi poster, 1923.*

Bavarians, the Bolshevik is at large! Out with him at election time! (Bavarian Volksparty)

▶ **SOURCE C** *Hitler, in* Mein Kampf:

Democracy... is the forerunner of Marxism. In fact the latter would not be conceivable without the former. Democracy is the breeding ground in which the bacilli of the Marxist world pest can grow and spread.

▶ **SOURCE D** *From a secondary text:*

During the early 1920s many civil servants happened to take their holidays on the anniversary of the Republic; a day on which they would otherwise have been expected to demonstrate their loyalty to the new state. The Republican flag was often not flown over public buildings. The Army always avoided flying it whenever possible... In the universities and grammar schools youths regarded the new democracy with contempt... Sixth-formers who used the Weimar Constitution for airgun practice were not untypical of their class and generation.

SECTION A: KU — GENERAL

1. In what ways was democracy guaranteed within the Weimar Constitution? (4)

2. Why was there considerable opposition to the Weimar Republic within Germany? (4)

3. To what extent was the most harmful opposition to the Weimar Republic from within the Weimar system itself? Explain your answer. (4)

SECTION B: EV — GEN/CREDIT

1. Are Sources B and C biased? Explain your answer. (4)

2. What similar and different ideas on democracy are expressed in Sources A, B and C? (4)

3. Do the sources accurately represent the range of attitudes to the Weimar system that existed in the early 1920s? Explain your answer. (4)

UNIT 3 · CONTEXT D ·
People and Power: Germany 1918–39
SPARTAKIST REVOLT, 1919–20

▶ **SOURCE A** *A Spartakist poster.*

The slogan reads 'Choose the Spartakists'. The figures in the poster are Weimar Assembly deputies

▶ **SOURCE B** *Rosa Luxemburg, Spartakist leader:*

Whenever a window-pane crashes to the pavement, or a tyre bursts in the street, our opponents at once look over their shoulders; their hair standing on end and pimply with gooseflesh, they whisper, 'Aha! Here comes Spartakus!' ... The Social Democrats deliberately misrepresent our socialist aims as banditry. They yell against revolts, murder and similar rubbish, but they mean socialism. But the game will not succeed ... Even if events should throw us back into those jails we have just left. The iron course of revolution cannot be held up. Our voice will sound loud and clear. The masses will understand us and they will turn all the more fiercely against those who speak against us.

In December 1918 the Spartakists rose in Berlin.

▶ **SOURCE C** *From a secondary text.*

The language of the German Communists ... was very violent and seemed to be encouraging immediate insurrection ... Actually Luxemburg saw it as the Party's task to educate the German masses by demonstrating the conservative nature of Ebert's Government. Only then, in her view, would they be roused to demand revolutionary action ... Once the fighting had started, however, she believed the workers' leaders ought not to desert them ... The rebels were crushed ... The new Defence Minister in Ebert's Government made use of Freikorps volunteer formations led by Imperial officers ... violently opposed to revolution. Luxemburg and Liebknecht were murdered by men of these units.

▶ **SOURCE D** *German newspaper extracts, January, 1919:*

The deaths of Luxemburg and Liebknecht were the proper reward for the blood bath they unleashed. The result of her own actions killed the woman. The day of judgment of Luxemburg and Liebknecht is over. Germany has peace; it can breathe again. The Spartakists were criminals pure and simple, who had lost a long time ago all power to distinguish good from evil!

SECTION A: KU — GENERAL

1 What were the aims of the Spartakist movement in Germany? (4)

2 Why did the Spartakists attempt to overthrow the German government in December 1918? (4)

3 How important a threat to law and order within Germany did the Spartakists present? Explain your answer. (4)

SECTION B: EV — GEN/CREDIT

1 How useful are Sources A and B as evidence of the aims and attitudes of the Spartakists in 1919? (4)

2 Do Sources B and C provide similar and consistent accounts of the ideals of Rosa Luxemburg? Explain your answer. (4)

3 To what extent are the views of the Spartakists put forward in Source D justified? Explain your answer. (4)

UNIT 3 · CONTEXT D
People and Power: Germany 1918–39
ECONOMIC PROBLEMS OF THE WEIMAR REPUBLIC

Financial problems in Germany 1918–23

▶ **SOURCE A** *German Mark against US dollar.*

July	1914	4.2 marks to $1
January	1919	8.9 marks to $1
January	1920	64.8 marks to $1
January	1921	64.9 marks to $1
January	1922	191.8 marks to $1
January	1923	17,927.0 marks to $1
August	1923	4,620,455.0 marks to $1

▶ **SOURCE B** *From a German novel:*

In 1923 I was advertising chief of a rubber factory. That was during the inflation. I had a monthly salary of 200 billion marks. We were paid twice a day, and then everybody had half an hour's leave so that he could rush to the stores and buy something before the next quotation on the dollar came out at which time the money would lose half its value.

▶ **SOURCE C** *German postage stamps.*

▶ **SOURCE D** *Hitler, writing in* Mein Kampf *(published 1924):*

The Government calmly goes on printing these scraps of paper because, if it stopped, that would be the end of the Government. Once the printing presses stopped — and that is the prerequisite for the stabilisation of the mark — the swindle would be brought to light ... Believe me, our misery will increase. The scoundrel will get by. The reason: because the State itself has become the biggest swindler and crook. A robbers' state! ... If the horrified people notice that they can starve on billions, they must arrive at this conclusion; we will no longer submit to a State which is built on the swindling ideas of the majority. We want a dictatorship ...

SECTION A: KU — GENERAL

1 Describe the growing financial problems within Germany between 1918 and 1923. (4)

2 What were the effects of the mounting financial crisis on economic and social life in Germany? (4)

3 How important was the financial crisis as a cause of government unpopularity in Germany in the early 1920s? Explain your answer. (4)

SECTION B: EV — GEN/CREDIT

1 How useful are Sources B and C as evidence of German financial problems in the 1920s? (4)

2 In what ways do Sources A, B and C give a consistent picture of the German economy in the early 1920s? (4)

3 To what extent were the views put forward in Source D supported by ordinary Germans in 1924? Explain the reasons for your answer. (4)

UNIT 3 · CONTEXT D ·
People and Power: Germany 1918–39
FORMATION / CHARACTER OF NATIONAL SOCIALISM

▶ **SOURCE A** *Account by Rudolf Diels, Head of Prussian political police, 27 February 1933:*

Shortly after my arrival at the burning Reichstag, the NSDAP leaders arrived ... As I entered Goering came towards me. His voice was heavy with emotion: 'This is the Communist revolt, they will start their attack now!'

Hitler, his face purple with agitation, shouted uncontrollably, as if he was going to burst: 'There will be no mercy now! Anyone who stands in our way will be cut down ... Every Communist official will be shot where he is found! The Communist deputies must be hanged this very night ... There will no longer be leniency for Social Democrats either!'

▶ **SOURCE B** *Extract from the Decree for the Protection of People and State, 28 February 1933:*

Article I: Restrictions on personal liberty and free expression of opinion including freedom of the press and the right of free assembly. Opening of suspicious mail and warrants for house searches are to be allowed for government officials.

The Reich Government may take over any German state where steps needed for keeping public order are not taken.

▶ **SOURCE C** *Historian's comment on the Decree:*

The suspension of civil rights contained in Article I provided a foundation for the use of terror and intimidation which was to follow. In particular it gave an excuse for the use of so-called 'protective custody' used by the Gestapo to jail people without trial.

▶ **SOURCE D** *Adapted from a secondary text:*

The election of 5 April did not give Hitler an absolute majority ... but the opposition was completely incapable of offering effective resistance. The Centre party had already shown itself willing to collaborate with Hitler ... The parties of the moderate right had been destroyed as an electoral force in the summer of 1933. The Communists were arrested or forced into hiding. Only the Social Democrats put a brave face on defeat. When on 23 March Hitler presented the Reichstag with an Enabling Law empowering him to rule by decree, the SPD was the only group to vote against it ... Hitler was master of Germany.

SECTION A: KU — GENERAL

1 Describe the main events in the Nazi takeover of power in Germany between February and March 1933. (4)

2 Explain how the Nazi seizure of power had affected German public life by April 1933. (4)

3 For what reasons was the Reichstag Fire a crucially important event for Nazism and Germany? (4)

SECTION B: EV — GEN/CREDIT

1 How useful is Source A as evidence about the attitudes of Nazi leaders towards political opponents within Germany? (4)

2 To what extent do Sources A and D show similar actions and attitudes on the part of the Nazi leaders? (3)

3 How accurately do the sources show the ruthlessness of the Nazis and the weakness of their political opponents in 1933? Fully explain. (5)

· UNIT 3 · CONTEXT D ·
People and Power: Germany 1918–39
NATIONAL SOCIALISM: MILITARISM, INTIMIDATION

▶ **SOURCE A** *A Nazi election poster.*

'Nazism: organised German nationalism'

▶ **SOURCE B** *Eye-witness, Nazi rally, 1932:*

There stood Hitler in a simple black coat ... a forest of swastikas and pennants swished up ... a roaring salute. His main themes: 'Out of parties will grow a nation ... the German nation.' He attacked the 'system' ('I want to know what there is left to be ruined in this state.') 'On the way here, socialists confronted me with a poster "Turn back Adolf Hitler". Thirteen years ago I was a simple unknown soldier. I went my way. I never turned back then. Nor shall I turn back now.' The speech over, there was roaring applause ... How many look up to him with touching faith as their saviour.

▶ **SOURCE C** *Eye-witness account by NSDAP sympathiser, February 1933:*

Torchlight procession of National Socialists and Stalhelm! A wonderfully elevating experience for all of us ... It was 10pm by the time the first torchlights came and more than 20,000 brownshirts (SA) followed one another like waves in the sea ... 'Three cheers for our Führer, our Chancellor, Adolf Hitler!' 'Down with the Republic' and 'The murderous reds have bloody hands!' ... There was a delegation of marching nationalist students ... A magnificent picture, the snow white, scarlet, moss-green and black colours, the fantastic berets, boots and gauntlets in the dancing light of the torches ... The swords, the flags ... We were drunk with enthusiasm, blinded by the light of the torches, enveloped in their vapour as in a cloud of sweet incense.

▶ **SOURCE D** *Account by SPD official, SA attack on SDP/union office, March 1933:*

The Nazis broke the big display windows and pushed into the building ... They opened fire inside the building with rifles and revolvers ... A 20 year old salesman was killed by a shot in the stomach. Union secretaries, employees, typists, salesgirls, were all driven together with cudgels, rifles, revolvers and daggers ... They were locked up for hours before being released with kicks and slaps.

SECTION A: KU — GENERAL

1 What main contributions did the SA make to the activities of the NSDAP? (3)

2 Why did Nazism appeal successfully to many German people? Fully explain your answer. (5)

3 How important was Adolf Hitler in the development of Nazism in Germany? Explain your answer. (4)

SECTION B: EV — GEN/CREDIT

1 How useful are Sources A and B as evidence of aims of the NSDAP? (4)

2 Do Sources B and C give similar or different views on the appeal of Nazism? Explain your answer. (4)

3 Does Source C or Source D more accurately represent typical Nazi methods? Explain your answer. (4)

UNIT 3 · CONTEXT D ·
People and Power: Germany 1918–39
CREDIT QUESTIONS: KU

1. *In November 1918, the state that Bismarck had founded collapsed. It was replaced by a most un-German Republic.*

   Describe how the Second Reich was succeeded by the German Republic set up on 9 November 1917. (4)

2. *'We want to erect a nation of Justice and Truth, based upon the equality of all human beings.'* (Friedrich Ebert, in a speech in February 1919)

   To what extent was the Weimar Republic formally established in 1919 in Germany, based upon justice, truth and equality? Explain your answer. (4)

3. *There were strong minorities, both to the nationalist right and the socialist left, that would have preferred dictatorship to the liberal democracy offered by the Wiemar system.*

   Choose **either** the Spartakist Revolt of 1919–20 **or** the Munich Putsch of November 1923. Fully describe and explain the causes which gave rise to the revolt, discuss the course of the rising, and its results and consequences. (8)
   For this question you should write a short essay of several paragraphs.

4. *The financial crises of 1923 and the late 1920s threatened to overwhelm the beleaguered and battered German Republic.*

   Was national economic failure the most important cause of the continuing unpopularity of the German Republic in the 1920s? Explain your answer. (4)

5. *'We never had enough money, many a time, pasting the placards for some world-shaking meeting, we lacked money to pay for the paste'* (NSDAP organiser talking of the early days of the Party in 1919)

   Explain how the National Socialist Party became the most powerful political party in Germany by the early 1930s. (4)

6. *'A strong national government can intervene in the liberties of the individual citizen without thereby weakening the ideals and principles of the German Reich.'* (Hitler, in Mein Kampf)

   Describe the ways in which the National Socialist government intervened in the civil liberties of people within Germany after 1933. (4)

APPENDIX A
SPECIMEN ANSWERS

1B6

· UNIT 1 · CONTEXT B ·
Changing Scotland/Britain, 1830s–1930s
PARLIAMENTARY REFORM — WOMEN'S SUFFRAGE

KU (General)

▶ANSWERS

▶NOTES

1 *Describe the methods used by Suffragettes in their campaigns for votes for women.*

The Suffragettes used methods which showed their protest at not having the vote. They tried to interrupt political meetings by heckling. Among the more dramatic methods of protest used, some Suffragettes drew attention to their cause by chaining themselves to railings near busy places like Downing Street and Buckingham Palace in London.

Some protests were deliberately violent, like smashing shop windows, or even setting fire to public buildings. Many Suffragettes were willing to be arrested and even suffer imprisonment for their principles. However not all Suffragette protests were violent. Like other political groups they organised peaceful rallies and public meetings to persuade others and further their cause.

A KU DESCRIPTION question

So describe ...

Use the sources to describe methods used.

Aim at giving as much information as you can.

Use your own knowledge. You cannot get full marks unless you do ...

2 *Why did some Suffragettes believe it necessary to use violence to be successful?*

The Suffragette leader Mrs Emmeline Pankhurst herself argued that violence made an impression on people by drawing clear attention to the cause. That is what she meant by saying that violence was a 'valuable argument' in politics. Because she was the leader, her views were taken up by many of her Suffragette followers.

Some Suffragettes also argued that Parliament had turned down the reasonable, peaceful arguments of women's suffrage movements for many years, so that hadn't worked.

Others might have argued that violence was in fact used by the authorities against women — for instance through forcible feeding of Suffragette hunger-strikers jailed for supporting the womens' cause, so Suffragettes' use of violence in turn was justified.

A KU EXPLANATION question

So explain ...

Use the sources to guide your answer.

Try to give as many reasons as you can.

Use your own knowledge
No full marks unless you do ...

▶ANSWERS

3 *To what extent was the First World War a turning-point in the campaign for votes for women? Fully explain your answer.*

The First World War was important in the votes for women campaign in a number of ways. Firstly the fact that one of the most powerful government ministers, Lloyd George actually directly asked the Suffragette leader to help the war effort was an important recognition of women's key role in British society.

Women served in dangerous jobs — as nurses working on or near the war-fronts: some served in hard and exhausting jobs previously done mainly by men — for instance as farmworkers in the Land Army. This impressed many men, including politicians and government leaders. It was their work in munitions factories that provided the argument in Parliament which led to the passing of the 1918 Representation Act giving women the right to vote for the first time.

While it would be wrong to say that it was only the war that brought women the vote, the war was nevertheless a turning-point in changing popular attitudes to women's suffrage.

▶NOTES

*A KU **JUDGMENT** question*

*So **make a judgment***

Use the sources to support your arguments

Use your own knowledge. You should know why by now!

End a judgment question by summing up your answer to the question

---

EV (General/Credit)

▶ANSWERS

1 *How useful are Sources B and E in showing the attitudes of their respective creators?*

Source B is a cartoon which shows the attitude of the cartoonist in a number of ways. The main point the cartoonist wants to make is that Suffragettes were violent — the woman admits to 'burning two pavillions and a church'.

The cartoonist uses humour to show how ridiculous the violent methods used by the women were. In Source E Lord Birkenhead gives his feelings away by showing that — in his opinion — women got the vote in 1918 by a type of trickery. In the debate on the 1918 Bill, MPs were tricked into allowing votes for women by firstly being persuaded to allow voting rights for wartime munition workers but, since most of these were women, the MPs couldn't change their decision.

It is clear from the words he used that Lord Birkenhead didn't approve of votes for women, which he calls a 'disaster'.

▶NOTES

*An EV question about the **VALUE** of sources*

Think about the type of source and of whether authorship is important

Pick out those things that show the author's feelings

Sometimes the actual words used can be important

▶ ANSWERS

▶ NOTES

2 Do Sources D and E agree or disagree on the reasons for women gaining the vote? Explain.

Source D and E agree that women gained the vote mainly because of their work in supporting Britain's war effort.

The sources agree that work done by women in the munitions industry was especially important. However, the sources disagree over the effect that women's war work had on other people. Source D claims that because of the impression made by their war work it was 'a foregone conclusion' that they would be given the vote. Source E suggests that, far from being a foregone conclusion, MPs were not all impressed by women's war work, and in the end passed the Bill giving women the vote only because the decision to reward all munition workers had already been taken and the Commons could not refuse women munitions workers the same rights as others.

An EV question asking you to **COMPARE** *sources*

Describe the ways in which the sources agree

... and disagree

Make sure that you make any necessary explanations in comparing the sources

3 How accurately do the sources represent the attitudes of people in Britain towards the idea of votes for women? Fully explain.

Sources B and E in different ways show clear opposition to votes for women. The cartoon (Source B) however is mainly making the point that what people disliked was the violent methods of some of the Suffragettes. This was quite a common feeling — even among some of the Suffragettes who preferred more peaceful campaigns.

Source C accurately sums up the WSPU attitude, showing that its leader was quite open in her belief that violence was certain to force change because it couldn't be ignored.

What this doesn't show, however, is the fact that Mrs Pankhurst had come to this conclusion only because other peaceful campaigns had been ignored by parliament.

It is doubtful if Lord Birkenhead accurately represents the feelings of most MPs with regard to votes for women, although parliament was cautious enough to give the vote only to women over thirty.

What none of the sources show however is the often violent attitude of men who intimidated female campaigners.

An EV question asking you to **compare the source with what you know** *about the topic*

Try to link the source with the background... What is the point of view of the author... Was this point of view typical?

Remember that the source might be inaccurate if it leaves out important matters

You need to decide whether the bias in this account shows the views of others accurately

· UNIT 2 · CONTEXT B ·
International Cooperation and Conflict, 1890s–1920s
EXPERIENCE OF WAR — CIVILIAN LIFE

KU (General)

▶ANSWERS

▶NOTES

1 *In what ways were men encouraged to join the armed forces during the First World War?*
Men were encouraged to join up in a number of ways.
   Everyone was encouraged to hate the Germans as evil and brutal enemies. This would help persuade men to join up and oppose the hated enemy.
   Men were encouraged to see enlisting in the forces as the best form of patriotism. In Source C wearing the 'King's uniform' is seen as something to be admired. At the same time, failure to join up was seen as cowardly and unmanly. Married men were encouraged to believe that the best way of protecting their families was to enlist.
   Fathers who did not do so would be faced with continuing shame as their children questioned them about what they did in the war.
   There were recruiting posters everywhere, some using the influence of war heroes like General Kitchener to try to persuade men to enlist. Even in the Music Halls, entertainers sung patriotic songs to encourage men to enlist.

*A KU **DESCRIPTIVE** question*

You are asked to describe how men were encouraged to join up

Use the sources: in this case you have to look beyond the posters to see how these 'encourage' recruitment

Aim at giving as much information as you can

Use your own knowledge. *You cannot get full marks unless you do*

2 *Why did the government try to change people's eating habits during the First World War?*
During the war food such as butter, meat and fish became more scarce. The two main ways in which the government tried to deal with growing shortages were, firstly, by introducing strict rationing of food in short supply, and secondly by trying to encourage people to eat less of these items. Source E, for instance, is asking people to eat less bread. Most of the wheat for making bread was brought in by ship. Allied merchant ships crossing the Atlantic were suffering heavy casualties at the hands of German U-boats. So, if less grain needed to be imported, the naval fleet would be helped. In fact, what the government wanted was for the ships to be carrying war materials like ammunition, rather than foodstuff.

*A KU **EXPLANATION** question*

*So **explain**...*

Use the sources to guide your answer

Refer to particular sources if this helps to explain your answer

Make sure you give as full an explanation as you can

Use your own knowledge. *No full marks unless you do...*

▶ANSWERS

3 *How important was it for the warring countries to organise the home front as well as win victories on the war front? Fully explain your answer.*

In the first place life had to be well organised within the warring countries so that a maximum number of young adult males could be freed from their normal work to serve in the armed forces. Since vast armies of millions of men were needed (Germany and France each had over two million regular soldiers in their armies, Russia many millions more), the whole country had to be reorganised.

In Britain, this task was so important that Lloyd George, the Munitions Minister in the early war years, took steps to persuade millions of women to take over jobs in industry, transport and farming, many of which had been done previously only by men.

The Defence of the Realm Act gave the government special powers to move workers into jobs which were important in the war.

It was also important to make sure that supplies of things like industrial raw materials, munitions and scarce foodstuffs were protected. Rationing and converting as much land as possible for food farming were carried out. The fact that one of the reasons why Germany had to surrender in 1918 was starvation among her people shows just how important success or failure on the home front was.

EV (General/Credit)

▶ANSWERS

1 *To what extent are Sources C and E useful evidence of how the authorities tried to influence people's lives in wartime Britain?*

Source C is a recruitment poster, so it gives a clear indication of the government's attempts to persuade people to enlist in the army. Posters were put on display in many public places, showing how the government tried to make sure that everyone got the message. In a similar way the public poster in Source E shows that the government tried to get everyone — men, women and children — to change their normal habits, and in this case change their diets, to help the war effort.

Source C shows that the government was willing to try to put pressure on people to do what it wanted. In this case males are being pressured by the thought that others might think them cowards or lacking in patriotism if they did not enlist. In Source E people are asked to think of the additional risks they cause to sailors by expecting them to carry wheat from overseas.

▶NOTES

*A KU **JUDGMENT** question*

You are asked to judge the importance of organising the home front

Use the sources to support the arguments you make

Always keep the question in mind: a judgment answer must make and support your argument

Use your own knowledge. *You must remember why by now!*

The question is about the 'warring countries' — so refer to countries other than Britain

▶NOTES

*An EV question asking about the **VALUE** of sources*

Read the question carefully — the value of the sources for what purpose?

Always make sure you indicate which source you are assessing

In a question like this one, which is asking about the effect of the sources on people, you must try to explain your answer carefully

At the end ask yourself 'Have I answered the question fully?'

▶ANSWERS

▶NOTES

2 *To what extent do Sources A and B give similar views of Germany and Germans?*

Both sources are very different in that one is a public poster, while the other shows one girl's private views of the Germans.

However both are similar in a number of ways. Both are clearly anti-German. Both show the Germans as wicked. Both sources are quite violent in their opposition to Germany.

While the views of Germany and Germans are therefore generally similar, the sources show different aspects of what is seen as German evil. In Source A the Germans are described as 'deceitful spies', while Source B shows the Germans as warlike, brutal and heartless, willing to attack the weak and defenceless.

An EV question asking you to ***COMPARE*** *sources*

So compare — and make sure you refer to both the sources involved

Describe and, if necessary, explain similarities in the sources

But remember also to describe/explain differences in the sources

'Have I answered the question fully?'

3 *How significant are the sources in showing the changing effects of the war on the home front in Britain?*

Sources A and C show the effects of propaganda against Germany in the earlier stages of the war. People were encouraged to hate the Germans, not simply as enemies, but as inhuman, cruel and barbaric beings.

The fact that even a little girl of twelve years of age can wish to kill all Germans (in a most brutal way) shows the effect of anti-German propaganda. In reality, people in Britain were often violently anti-German. Shops owned by people with German-sounding names were attacked in the early days of war. The Royal Family changed its German name to 'Windsor' to avoid unpopularity.

Sources D and E show how the continuance of the long drawn-out war affected both the government and the people in Britain. Source D is significant in that it not only shows the types of food in short supply, but it clearly shows how shortages were spreading by 1918. The poster in Source E shows indirectly the significant effect of the German U-boat campaign against Allied merchant ships. The appeal to save wheat underlines the fear that, while the war on the western front was being won, the Germans could still have forced the British to surrender by starving the country of essential war materials and food.

An EV question asking you to look at the ***source*** *and* ***what you know about the topic***

The sources are propaganda: explain why this is important

Tell what you know about the topic with reference to the sources

Explain how the sources help us to see the real historical situation

The source . . .

. . . real situation at that time

'Have I used all the sources, as the question asked?'

UNIT 3 · CONTEXT D
People and Power: Germany 1918–39
CHARACTERISTICS OF WEIMAR: OPPOSITION

KU (General)

▶ANSWERS

▶NOTES

1 *In what ways was democracy guaranteed within the Weimar Constitution?*

Democracy was guaranteed mainly by giving all German people over the age of twenty the right to vote in both Reichstag and State Parliament elections in Germany.

By law every citizen had the right to a guarantee of personal liberty, and could express his or her opinions freely, without the fear of arrest or imprisonment.

The most powerful and popular political parties, the Social Democrat and Liberal parties, were both fully behind the democractic ideals of the Weimar Constitution.

The fact that these parties made up a majority of deputies in the Reichstag seemed to guarantee the democratic rights set out in the Constitution.

*A KU **DESCRIPTIVE** question*

Describe how the Constitution guaranteed democracy

Use the sources to show how ...

Make as many points as you can

Use your own knowledge. You cannot get full marks unless you do ...

2 *Why was there considerable opposition to the Weimar Republic within Germany?*

While the parties supporting the Weimar Constitution were in a majority in the Reichstag, there were strong and determined opponents of Weimar in the country. These opponents came from both the nationalist right-wing and socialist and communist left-wing extremist parties. They viewed the Weimar government — which was usually made up of representatives from different parties in a coalition — as weak. Parties like the Nazis on the right and the KPD on the left both wanted more dictatorial, stronger governments. Both opposed democracy which was so basic to Weimar.

The inability of the early Weimar governments to tackle the massive financial and economic problems left by the war led to growing unpopularity and further opposition.

The army had never fully accepted the Weimar system. While the army was willing to support law and order within the country, it tolerated, rather than supported, the Weimar leadership, which, like the Nazis and other nationalist parties, it regarded as too tolerant of Marxist socialists.

*A KU **EXPLANATION** question*

*So **explain** ...*

Using the sources will help guide and shape your answer

Aim at giving as many reasons as possible

Use your own knowledge. No full marks unless you do ...

▶ANSWERS

▶NOTES

3 *To what extent was the most harmful opposition to the Weimar Republic from within the Weimar system itself? Explain your answer.*

Both the army and the civil service were less than wholehearted in their support for the Republic. This was a very serious situation, since the Republican government depended greatly upon these groups for its authority and even for its survival.

The extremist parties which were totally opposed to the Republic were capable of using extreme violence against the government. The armed force of the army was therefore essential to the authority and control of the government. In the period following the end of the war Germany was a very violent society. Political assassinations of important members of the Weimar government took place. In 1920 a group of Marxist revolutionaries called the Spartakists were suppressed only with the support of the army and the nationalist Friekorps soldiers. In 1920 another right-wing putsch led by a retired civil service chief — the Kapp Putsch — was again suppressed with difficulty.

In 1923 elements of the army leadership sided with Hitler and other nationalist groups, only to be finally put down by government supporters in the army.

In the end it was the growing political power of the NSDAP rather than army or civil service weakness which brought down the Weimar Republic.

*A KU **JUDGMENT** question*

Think carefully about this type of question — You are being asked to judge what was the most harmful type of opposition ...

There was opposition from many different quarters

Dislike of the Republic did not always lead to outright opposition

... the army didn't like the Republic

... but didn't want its removal

Use your own knowledge. *Remember why?*

If it is appropriate, make a final judgment

EV (General/Credit)

▶ANSWERS

▶NOTES

1 *Are Sources B and C biased? Explain your answer.*

Both sources were created by Nationalist groups who hated Socialists in general and Marxists or Communists in particular. The bias in Source B is shown mainly in the way the poster emphasises and exaggerates the violence of the Bolsheviks or Communists in Germany, who are seen to be willing to destroy whole cities like Munich and Berlin. The Bolshevik is shown as having Asian or Russian features and dress, and is shown as evil and sinister.

Source C was written by Hitler and was printed and sold throughout Germany. The purpose of *Mein Kampf* as the book was called was to turn people against both the Communists and the Weimar Republic. The bias is shown by the language used, for instance 'the Marxist world pest' which suggests Communism was a kind of disease finding a 'breeding ground' in the weak Weimar Republic.

*An EV question asking about the **VALUE** of sources*

Make sure that you clearly identify which source you are discussing

Bias can be shown in a number of ways — so try to be as thorough in your answer as possible

Explaining the purpose of a source (in this case Mein Kampf) often helps explain the bias involved

Ask yourself 'Have I answered the question as fully as possible?'

▶ANSWERS

▶NOTES

2 *What similar and different ideas on democracy are expressed in Sources A, B and C?*
In Source A democracy is shown as being at the root of guaranteed freedom and liberty for all Germans, and is claimed to be the foundation of equality and the right to a share of decision-making and power for all citizens.

In Source C Hitler, on the other hand, argues that democracy encourages and protects Marxism. It is the very freedom which the Weimar Republic guaranteed that allowed Communism to spread throughout the country.

Source B makes a similar point about the dangers of Communism, but also makes the different point that through their democractic rights the German people could vote in anti-Communist representatives and thus control the spread of Marxism.

An EV question asking you to ***COMPARE*** *sources*

While you might need to explain points about each source, always remember that you need to make comparison between sources

*Compare by showing similarities **and** differences*

'Have I answered the question as fully as possible?'

3 *Do the sources accurately represent the range of attitudes to the Weimar system that existed in the early 1920s? Explain your answer.*
While Source A shows the attitude of those who were generally in favour of the Weimar system, it does not indicate what the German people as a whole felt.

Source D suggests that the army and even the government's own civil service felt little real support for the Weimar Republic. However, it must be borne in mind that the army did support the government at crucial times when internal revolution from both the Communists and the Nationalists looked likely to pull the government down.

The views expressed in Sources B and C are those of right wing nationalist opinion, which was very anti-Weimar, but not necessarily typical of German public opinion as a whole.

What the sources fail to show accurately is the fact that attitudes to Weimar changed during the 1920s.

When financial crisis arose, as in the early and late 1920s, the popularity of the Weimar government fell. There was a spell in the mid 1920s when the economy and Germany's international reputation both improved, and the Weimar Republic was reasonably popular.

An EV question asking you to look at the ***sources*** *in the light of* ***your knowledge*** *of the topic*

The question is about accuracy of the sources as evidence of how people thought at the time. So look at the source . . .

. . . and think of the real situation at the time

The sources . . .

. . . the real situation

Sources might be inaccurate not only in what they show — but in what they leave out

'Have I answered the question as fully as possible?'

CREDIT QUESTIONS (KU)

Context 1A

▶ANSWERS

▶NOTES

2 From the mid eighteenth century onwards, Britain was increasingly transformed by what came to be called the First Industrial Revolution.
Taking the example of the textile industry, discuss the main results of technological change during the eighteenth and nineteenth centuries in Britain. (4)
 In the middle of the eighteenth century, spinning and weaving — the two main processes — were carried out in the main by farmers and their families who did the work in their homes.
 By the later part of the century, and increasingly in the nineteenth century, spinning and weaving was done in factories.
 This change was in itself a result of the increased use of machine technology. Inventions like the Spinning Jenny and Samuel Crompton's 'Mule' could spin thread on many spindles at once, and were most efficient when driven by water-power. The first textile factories were built near rivers, so that large water mills could provide the power to drive the new machines. Factories were called 'mills' for this reason, although, by the end of the eighteenth century, machines driven by steam engines were more common.
 The flax used in linen making was difficult to work with on the new machines, so a new textile, cotton, imported from America, took over as the main cloth produced in Britain.
 As power machinery was used in weaving as well as spinning, skilled handloom weavers were increasingly unemployed, causing much hardship.
 Perhaps the most striking change brought about by technology was the growth of industrial areas devoted to cotton production. Cities like Manchester, and, in Scotland, towns like Paisley and, on a smaller scale, New Lanark grew in population and importance because of their cotton mills.

*A KU **DESCRIPTION** question*

*Results of technological change were complex, so try to be **thorough** in your answer*

There are more and less obvious results of technological change ... changes in how the industry was organised

... changes in types of machines
... and how machines were driven

... changes in type of cloth used

... changes affecting workers

... economic and population changes

Ask 'Have I answered the question as fully as possible?'

Context 1B

▶ANSWERS

▶NOTES

5 'The working class are determined to govern themselves and will not be hoodwinked by any class or class interests.'
How important was the Second Reform Act of 1867 in bringing about political democracy in Britain? Explain your answer. (4)
 The Second Reform Act of 1867 doubled from 1 to 2 millions the number of people who could vote in parliamentary elections.
 All male householders and even lodgers paying £10 or more in rent in the burghs, and in the counties people who leased land at a cost of at least £12 annually were given the vote.

*A KU **JUDGMENT** question*

Make sure you understand the question ... it is not just about effects of the Act ...

Make sure you provide basic information about the Act

▶ ANSWERS

In a corresponding change, the right to return MPs was taken away from burghs with few voters and the 45 seats acquired were given to larger burghs with 10,000 or more voters.

The changes were seen as being very important at the time.

One writer called the Act 'A leap into the dark'. However, there was little obvious change in terms of the type of MPs elected to parliament. There were no working class MPs.

Although the newly formed Liberal Party took most working class votes in the election of 1868, the party represented middle, and even reforming upper, class as well as working class voters.

Nevertheless the Act was seen by political parties as the beginning of popular democracy in Britain. The Liberal and Conservative Parties, formed at the time of the Act, were national parties, with carefully worked out policies which would appeal to a mass electorate made up of different social classes. The parties were backed up by a national organisation, to ensure people had a voice in the party, and to increase popular support in the country.

Although the mass electorate was still not in existence in 1867, the beginnings of popular democracy were.

▶ NOTES

Give as much information as you can ... if you are not sure if something is relevant — put it in anyway

Always think back to the question ... You are discussing importance of the Act for popular democracy

How important was it at the time?

What about the long-term importance?

... on political life and political parties

... on the 'popular' nature of politics

Sum up your answer if possible. 'Have I answered as fully as I can?'

Context 1C

▶ ANSWERS

1 The last 100 years have seen persistent migration within Britain and from Britain to other countries.
Discuss the causes of either migration within Britain or emigration from Scotland during the period from 1880 to the present day. (4)

Causes of migration within Britain have varied from time to time over the last century. In the late nineteenth century, movement tended to be from rural areas into the growing towns and cities, although the larger migrations from country to town had taken place earlier in the century.

This type of migration was caused by the need to find employment. Jobs were often hard to find in increasingly mechanised farming, but were usually plentiful in new industries like — in the later nineteenth century — shipbuilding, heavy engineering or steelmaking.

There was considerable seasonal migration of workers during the nineteenth and twentieth centuries. For instance Irish labourers came to Scotland for farm work at harvesting times. Many came also to work on building projects. A number stayed on in the country, and cities like Glasgow had a fair Irish and Highland population.

In the second half of the twentieth century the movement of people from country to town was to some extent reversed with the building of New Towns such as East Kilbride and Livingston. These towns were designed to provide jobs — usually in modern engineering industry — comfortable housing and good local amenities.

Many people were persuaded to move from older industrial and business centres like Glasgow, Edinburgh and Dundee to find work and housing in the attractive New Towns.

▶ NOTES

*A KU **EXPLANATION** question*

If there is a choice in the question make sure you think before you choose

In this case the choice is causes of migration within Britain

Causes can be complex: try to be **thorough**

... the need to have a job

... how this would lead to migration

... causes of different types of migration

Always think back to the question ... You need to discuss causes in the nineteenth and twentieth centuries.

Remember it is causes you have to explain ... don't simply describe

'Have I answered as fully as I can?'

Context 2B

▶ANSWERS

▶NOTES

3A We are the dead. Short days ago, we lived, felt dawn, saw sunset glow. Loved and were loved. And now we lie, in Flanders Field.

Why did war on the western front result in appalling and unprecedented casualties and loss of life? (8)

For this question you should write a short essay of several paragraphs.

The First World War was indeed a world-wide struggle. It involved massive armies, and, was — in terms of the numbers of people involved in the conflict — unprecedented.

Russia, Germany and France had armies of several million men. Even Britain — which still regarded her Royal Navy as the 'senior service' — eventually conscripted an army of well over one million. Given the scale of the conflict, massive casualties were inevitable.

The war lasted much longer than was at first expected. Many thought the war would last only months — the general belief in August 1914 was that it would be 'over by Christmas'. It was felt that the great armies would clash in two or three major set battles and defeat or victory would follow.

However, instead of a short 'war of movement', a long-drawn out 'war of attrition' with both sides pounding away at each other, and with continuing casualties, took over on the western front.

In addition to this continuous loss, there were massive casualties at battles like Verdun, the Somme, and the battles at Ypres. Each of these contests lasted for several months, so the number of casualties was appalling.

The methods and the technology used both in day-to-day trench warfare and in the great set-piece battles contributed to the growing casualties. The most effective weapons were defensive. The machine-gun probably accounted for more losses than any other single weapon.

Commanders persisted in the belief that artillery bombardment of enemy trenches before the infantry attacked would destroy the defences. On the first day of the Battle of the Somme, following the most massive bombardment of enemy trenches, 60,000 British infantry-men died — most cut down by German machine-guns.

The ordinary conditions of life in the trenches caused many to be invalided out of the struggle through complaints like 'trench feet' caused by the wet conditions. Some were blinded by mustard gas grenades, some suffocated in trench collapses during shelling. Some suffered shell-shock, and broke down mentally under the appalling strain.

Because of the unwillingness of the commanders to vary their tactics, men's lives continued to be thrown away, often for little or no territorial or strategic gain. The situation did not change until the end of the war came.

*A KU **EXPLANATION** question*

*This is an **extended answer** question*

*Be even more **thorough** with this type of question*
Clearly there are many reasons for the horrendous casualty rates

... The sheer scale of the conflict

*Provide **explanation**, not just description*

... The length of the war

... The nature of the fighting

... The large set-piece battles

*Provide **explanation**, not just description*

... The technology of warfare

Explanation

... The tactics used in battle

Give facts where you can

... Conditions on the western front

Explanation

'Have I answered as fully as I can?'

APPENDIX B
GLOSSARY

Page 1 **hey day** the best time
crossing-sweepers people who kept roads clean

Page 3 **plutocrat** a very wealthy person
budget yearly changes in laws on financial matters, eg tax payment
supertax high rate of income tax paid only by the wealthiest

Page 4 **financial 'crash'** collapse in value of currency (money)
business slump reduction in amount of business and trade
period collections items all belonging to a particular past time
archive place where historical records can be found

Page 8 **party** person

Page 10 **unconditional neutrality** taking no part, siding with no one in war
sanctioned gave authority for
Chancellor government leader
proclamation official announcement
Cabinet group of most important government ministers
ultimatum final demand (for Germany to pull out of Belgium)
Kaiser German emperor
press newspapers
proffered hand offer of friendship
insinuates hints
aloof from away from

Page 11 **commerce** trade

Page 12 **civilians** ordinary people at home, not soldiers
bereavements mourning those lost in the war
productivity amount produced by
urban city or town-dwelling
Central Powers Germany and Austria-Hungary
Freikorps voluntary armed groups formed to oppose communism

Page 13 **reformers** those working for what they believed were improvements
social security aid and support for people in need
initiative ability to act independently

Page 14 **dole-money** unemployment payments
devious cunning and deceitful

Page 20 **tenants** people who rent farmland from a landowner
improvers landowners who introduced more modern farming
cottars people who worked for tenant-farmers or landowners
dispossess drive out
beggary poverty

Page 21 **the state of manufactures** the state of local industry
muslin fine cotton cloth

Page 22 **wattled** put together in the form of a frame
'sell themselves for passage' agreeing to work as temporary bond-servants in return for paid passage to their destinations
'situations will be fixed on' jobs will be arranged

Page 23 **radical unrest** public protest by those wishing to force political change
radical someone who wants sweeping political change
pensioners government office-holders, paid annually
'kept a military order' in orderly lines
representation right to be represented by a Member of Parliament
entreat ask
'read the Riot Act' ordered troops in to restore public order

Page 24 **putrefy** decay
defiled dirty

Page 25 **'returns a Member'** elects a Member of Parliament
nominated selected
delegate representative
versed experienced
Dean of Guild leading magistrate in town council
Bailie leader of the town council

Page 27 **economising** making good use of
pastoral farming sheep or cattle farming

Page 28 **8d** eight old pence
1s one shilling
steerage having no private cabin or reserved space

Page 29	**insanitary** unhealthy, unhygienic **slum houses** dirty, decaying or unhealthy housing **compelled** forced **enclosures** fenced-off areas	Page 39	**sick club** insurance providing money in times of sickness absence from work **parish doctor** doctor appointed to look after the poorest people **disproportionate amount** much larger share **pawn** deposit personal property in exchange for temporary cash loan
Page 30	**taper** candle **hews** cuts from coal-face		
Page 31	**franchise** the right to vote **'exercise power'** take over government **party government** organisation of control of political party **constituency** area with right to return an MP to parliament	Page 40	**exercise power** hold government power **hoodwinked** misled or tricked **householders** people who rent houses **democracy** sharing political rights among people
Page 32	**heckled** interrupted **deplored** condemned, opposed **rallied** supported **'a foregone conclusion'** a future certainty **subtle** crafty **yielded** given in	Page 41	**jumble** mixed pile **treasury money** money provided by the government **contractor** builder
		Page 42	**domestic service** work as servant in (usually) large private house **'labour displaced'** workers no longer required
Page 33	**hovels** small, dirty houses **Patron** chief supporter **HMS** Her Majesty's Ship **shieling** farm cottage **kindred** family **fortified** protected **seer** someone who could foretell the future **'degenerate lord'** cruel, inhuman landowner **paupers** people without jobs or money	Page 43	**struck** went on strike **tanner** sixpenny piece **excited** brought about **offensive weapon** means of achieving (trade union) purposes **capitalism** private owners of business and industry
		Page 45	**Edict of Fraternity** declaration of brotherhood **resented** were unhappy about **inevitable** unavoidable **Constitution** rules by which the country is governed **French Ambassador** French government representative in another country **recover stability** settle **'the ultimate issue of the war'** who would win the war **'permanently enlisted'** in full time service **forge** manufacture/make
Page 34	**pauper** person without money or a job **infirm** weak, unwell **able-bodied** able to work **degradation** humiliation, shame **bastille** prison **deter** discourage **desolate** miserable		
Page 36	**exhibited** put on show **assumed** taken on **'macadamised'** tarred		
Page 37	**frigate** a type of small battleship **component structures** parts (of the ship) **subsidies** help in the form of cash or loans	Page 46	**contained** kept under control **auxiliaries** troops from allied countries **harassment** attacks
Page 38	**domestic service** jobs as household servants **commerce** business **'the professions'** eg medicine, law, teaching **'precision engineering jobs'** jobs which demand extremely accurate work **executive** management	Page 47	**eclipse** loss of importance **policy** course of action **militarism** warlike aggression, reliance on armed force

Page 48 ***Kaiser*** German emperor
'dead-on' heading directly
pith real point
'sabre-rattling' aggressive, threatening
'place in the sun' a place among the leading world colonial powers
inflammatory tending to stir up trouble

Page 49 ***pro-Slav*** supporting the interests of the Slavic people
'facilities for crossing the Bosnian border' agreement with border guards to allow them to cross the border
outrage disgraceful crime
implicated in involved in
mobilised prepared to fight
Chancellor government leader
ultimatum final demand
chief objects main aims
appropriate episode reasonable excuse for

Page 50 ***artillery bombardment*** shelling
stalemate situation where both sides are unable to advance
'Fritz' the Germans
parapet front defences of trench
density thickness

Page 51 ***enlisted*** joined (the armed forces)
'wearing the King's uniform' belonging to the armed forces

Page 53 ***fugitive*** person in hiding
reparations money Germany had to pay to make good war damage
affirm declare formally
Kaiser German emperor
intervention interference
reminiscent remindful

Page 54 ***policies*** course of action
vessels ships
neutrals countries taking neither one side nor the other
belligerents countries at war
'singularly in unison' joined in common cause
referendum on national vote on the question of
policy of 'isolation' staying clear of international involvement

Page 55 ***covenenant*** document listing terms of a broad agreement
'deemed wise and effectual' considered to be sensible and likely to be effective
expansionist ambitions desire to extend territories
economic sanctions withdrawal of trade links
military and naval measures use of force to back up sanctions

Page 57 ***universal military service*** requiring every adult male to serve in the armed forces
'adhere to this unconditionally' stand by an agreement
annex take over possession
psychological rearmament need to rebuild confidence (of the German people)

Page 58 ***incredible*** unbelievable
isolatated left alone
'campaign of eastern expansion' conquest of states to Germany's east

Page 59 ***platoon*** body of soldiers working as a unit
evacuees children moved from towns and cities to safer areas

Page 60 ***fatalities*** people killed
vapourised destroyed with no remaining trace
radioactive giving off harmful rays
the 'Superfortress' the US aircraft which had dropped the atom bomb
arsenal stock of weapons
morality consideration of right and wrong
datum/data fact/facts

Page 61 ***Colonial powers*** European countries which had overseas colonies
'at ministerial level' between government leaders
'accelerate withdrawal of our forces' pull troops out more quickly

Page 62 ***monopoly*** sole power
airlift taking in supplies by aircraft
fascist (in this case) mainly Nazi party supporters
infiltrators (in this case) people entering the country secretly with evil intent

Page 63 **UNO** United Nations Organisation
scourge curse
reaffirm faith re-state a belief in
fundamental human rights basic rights of all human beings
veto the right to stop particular actions or decisions from being taken
ultimate final
diplomacy negotiation
Leninist doctrine policy/belief of Lenin (founder of Soviet Union)
'concept of a world society' believing in one world society (as opposed to Capitalist and Communist worlds)
Truman doctrine policy/belief of President Truman of the USA
'putting political pressure on' forcing countries into certain actions or policies
just fair
anarchy disorder
chaos confusion

Page 64 **acute crisis** serious incident/development
rendered made
'provocative change in the status quo' change in the existing state of things deliberately intended to stir up trouble
quarantine ban
instituted brought in
retaliatory response counter-attack, hitting back
reconcile themselves to come to accept
deterrent to means of preventing

Page 66 **high protein count** plenty of protein (an important food type)
preferred jobs better, more responsible jobs
Southerners Americans living in slave-owning southern states
Northerners Americans living in non-slave-owning northern states
humiliation shame
endeavoured tried
abolitionist person against slave-ownership
forfeit give up
humanest kindest
deliverance release

Page 67 **Southern Confederacy** federation of slave-owning southern states
advocates supporters
dissolved broken up
precipitately rashly
abolitionist person against slave-ownership
deprecated hated

Page 68 **Platte** River Platte (in Nebraska, Wyoming and Colorado)
prairie lands treeless, grass-covered plains of the West
'lunches put up' lunches served
provident taking care for the future

Page 69 **stampede** uncontrolled rush (of people)
prospectors people in search of gold
'three-pronged invasion' attack by three armed groups

Page 70 **responsible government** government responsible to the (Indian) people
transfer of power giving of power to the people
viceroy a British ruler of India
wielded possessed
barrister lawyer
wily crafty
exploitation using for selfish purposes

Page 71 **partition** separation of Hindu and Moslem areas in India
disruptive causing upset or disorder
Viceroy British ruler of India
chaos disorder
attribute failure to put blame into
instituted created
progressive measures forward-looking actions

Page 72 **artillery reserves** stocks of shells
conscription forced entry into the army
complement full number
nurtured taken care of
pince-nez spectacles
duped tricked
bourgeoisie middle classes
revolutionary crisis crisis making revolution unavoidable
proletarian working class

Page 73 **disturbances** riots and protests
anarchy state of total disorder
calamitous disastrous
abdicate the throne give up (position as ruler)

Page 74 **'capitalist plunderers'** businessmen and industrialists who made greater profits because of the war
capital punishment execution (of any deserters)
Soviets councils of workers and soldiers' representatives
SRs members of the Social Revolutionaries Party
thwart prevent
incited encouraged

Page 75 **offered his resignation from** offered to give up his position in
profound conviction deep belief
insurrection uprising
underground in hiding
government apparatus system of government
Soviets councils of workers and soldiers' representatives
cessation ending
bankrupt in this sense the word means 'finished'

Page 76 **SR** Social Revolutionaries Party
extermination destruction
bourgeoisie middle classes
Cheka communist secret police
requisitioning bands soldiers sent to take grain from peasants

Page 77 **capitalist system** private ownership of business and industry
rural in country areas
offensive attack
Kulaks rich peasant-farmers
Secretariat the Communist Party office whose task it was to organise all party business. Since the Party and the government were closely linked in Soviet Russia, the Party Secretariat was virtually a government office under Stalin
defamed destroyed
GPU Stalin's secret police
unscrupulous dishonest
Okrhana old Tsarist state secret police whose real task was to crush political opposition to the government
purges removal of opposition

Page 78 **state planning** planning for increased industrial output
consumer goods goods which can be bought by the public
heavy industry eg iron and steel, coal, engineering industries
collectivisation all farming land within a locality (or district) was brought under the control of the local soviet which organised all work activities on this local collective farm
NEP New Economic Policy which replaced war communism
'the underground' secret revolutionary movement
GPU Stalin's secret police

Page 80 **Kaiser** German emperor
abdication (Kaiser) giving up the throne
SPD German Social Democratic Party
consolidate make certain of
Hohenzollerns family name of German Kaisers
besmirched stained

Page 81 **ultimatum** final demand
unanimous co-operation a willingness of all to work together

Page 82 **constitution** rules by which a country is governed
universal suffrage all adults being allowed the vote
dictatorship rule by one person or one political party
Marxism communism
conceivable possible
bacilli disease organisms

Page 83 **Spartakists** German communist group led by Karl Liebknecht
Weimar Assembly parliament of the German Republic (at Weimar)
banditry unlawful actions
SPD German Social Democratic Party
insurrection uprising, rebellion
Freikorps volunteer groups raised to oppose communism in Germany

Page 84 **inflation** time of rapidly rising prices
'next quotation on the dollar' the German mark was frequently re-valued against the US dollar
'scraps of paper' (in this case) bank notes

Page 85 **NSDAP** National Socialists; German Nazi Party
Reichstag Parliament building in Berlin
deputies elected representatives in the Reichstag
leniency mercy
Social Democrats leading moderate socialist party in Parliament (SDP)
intimidation bullying
absolute overall
collaborate co-operate
SPD German Social Democratic Party

Page 86 **NSDAP** National Socialists; German Nazi Party
saviour the man who would save (the German nation)
elevating uplifting
Stalhelm ex-servicemen's movement in Germany
SPD German Social Democratic Party
cudgels clubs

ACKNOWLEDGMENTS

The Author and Publisher would like to thank the following for their valuable assistance and for their permission to reproduce copyright material, some of which has been adapted or translated.

▶ **ILLUSTRATIONS**

Associated Newspapers plc, cartoonist David Low (**61** A); Bilderdienst Suddeutscher Verlag (**82** B); Deutsche Bundespost (**84** C); Dundee District Libraries Photographic Collection (**29** E, **36** D, **41** B); Express Newspapers plc (**3** 5, **40** E); Farmers Weekly (**34** C); Fotomas Index (**7** left, **21** D); Greater London Photography Library (**1** 2); Hamlyn Publishing Group Ltd (**53** D); Heinemann Educational Books Ltd (**64** C, **71** A); Hoover Institution on War, Revolution and Peace, Stanford University (**72** A, **76** A, **78** A/B); Hulton-Deutsch (**3** 7, **14** left/right, **12** B, **29** C, **31** B, **36** F, **46** D, **57** D); Illustrated London News (**34** C, **40** A); Trustees of the Imperial War Museum (**11** C, **38** C, **50** A, **51** B/C, **52** E, **59** A/C); Institute of Contemporary History and Wiener Library Ltd (**86** A); International Instituut voor Sociale Geschiedenis (**83** A); The Labour Party (**7** right); Longman Group UK Ltd and C.C.C.P. (**58** B); The Mansell Collection (**8** top, **23** D, **25** D, **28** A, **30** C, **42** D); G. Kordas (**84** C); A.G. Nicolson (**37** A); G. Outram & Co. Ltd (**3** 5); Popperfoto (**12** E, **74** A); Punch Publications Ltd (**2** 6, **8** lower, **13** C, **24** C, **32** B, **36** A, **54** A, **80** A); Rheinischer Merkur/Christ und Welt (**81** C); Sheffield City Libraries (**30** E); University of Reading, Institute of Agricultural History and Museum of English Rural Life (**27** A); Utah State Historical Society (**68** A); Wyoming State Archives, Museums and Historical Department (**69** A).

▶ **EXTRACTS**

Edward Arnold (Publ.) Ltd: A History of Scotland by I. McPhail (**25** C, **33** D, **42** E), British Economic & Social History 1700–1970 by R.L. Tames (**29** D, **21** C); E.J. Arnold: A Course Book in British Social and Economic History from 1760 by P.F. Speed (**37** D); Batsford: Health and Hygiene by L. Rose (**24** D), Radicals and Reformers by P. Lane (**32** A), Roads by H. Bodey (**36** C/D/E), Employment by R. Lobban (**38** B/D/F, **39** C(i)), Europe since 1945 by P. Lane (**61** C, **62** D); Cambridge University Press: The British Welfare State 1900–1950 by Sydney Wood (**41** C); Cassell Ltd: The Kerensky Memoirs by A. Kerensky; Century: Mein Kampf by A. Hitler (**84** D); Collins: A Century of the Scottish People by T.C. Smout (**22** A, B, **41** A, **42** A, **42** B), Foreign Affairs 1886–1916 by M. Morgan (**47** C); Andre Deutsch Ltd: Russia in Revolution by H.E. Salisbury (**76** B); Hansard (Parliamentary Copyright): speech by Harold Wilson 16/01/68 (**61** D); Heinemann Publishers (Oxford) Ltd: A Map History of the Modern World by B. Catchpole (**58** A, **64** B, **71** B), Britain, Europe & the World by A. Edwards and G. Bearman (**28** B, **48** D), The Origins of the First World War by L. Trainer (**49** A); Holmes McDougall: Russia in Revolution by J.L. Taylor (**77** C); Trustees of the Imperial War Museum: With a Machine Gun to Cambrai by G. Coppard (**50** C); International Thomson Ltd: Britain between the Wars 1918–1940 by C.L. Mowat (**53** E, **70** B), Versailles and After by R.B. Henig (**58** D); ITV Books: The Wild West by R. May (**68** C, **69** B/C/E); Jane's Information Group: World War One by R. Hoare (**50** B); Michael Joseph: The Time of My Life by Denis Healey (**63** C); Alfred A. Knopf Inc.: The Genesis of the World War by H.E. Barnes (**49** E); Leeds Mercury, 16 October 1830 (**21** E); Longman Group UK Ltd: Scotland in the Days of Burns by H. Shapiro (**20** B), The French Revolution by M. Rosenthal (**45** D), World War One by S. Gibbons (**51** D, **54** B), An Illustrated History of Modern Europe by D. Richards (**58** C, **61** B, **62** C), The Making of America by B. Beacroft (**68** D, **69** D), Modern Russia by J. Robottom (**74** C, **75** C, **76** D, **78** D/E); Executors of Lord Selwyn Lloyd: "Suez 1956" by H.S. Lloyd (**63** E); McGraw-Hill Book Company: A History of American Life and Thought by N.M. Blake (**67** C); Macmillan Education Ltd: Weimar and the Rise of Hitler by A. Nicholls (**82** D, **85** D); Macmillan Inc: the Kerensky Memoirs by A. Kerensky (**74** D); Thomas Nelson & Sons Ltd: The Monkland Tradition by T.R. Miller (**37** B); The New American Library Ltd: The Rise and Fall of Nazi Germany by T. Jarman (**82** A); Northern College of Education: The Civilian War by M. Cuthbert (**59** B); Oxford University Press: A Portrait of Europe by M. Roberts (**46** C), Truman Speaks by H. Truman (**60** C), World Affairs from the Russian Revolution to the Present by E. Rayner, R. Stapley and J. Watson (**63** B, **64** D), Germany 1866–1945 by G.A. Craig (**84** A), English History 1914–45 by A.J.P. Taylor (**60** D, **70** A), Rosa Luxemburg by P. Nettl (**83** D); Pan: The Rise and Fall of the Third Reich by W.L. Shirer (**57** A); Pelican: My Life by Leon Trotsky (**75** D); Penguin Books Ltd: A History of Scotland by J.D. Mackie (2nd ed. 1978) (**42** C), England in the Twentieth-Century by D. Thomson (**71** B/D), The First World War by A.J.P. Taylor (**49** D), Britain — Twentieth Century by M.C. Borer (**32** D, **36** B); Random House Publishing: And Quiet Flows the Don by M. Sholokov (**72** C); Secker & Warburg: The Rise and Fall of the Third Reich by W. Shirer (**80** D); Sidgwick & Jackson: The Day before Yesterday by A. Thompson (**62** A/D); The Times, 16 September 1889 (**43** C); United Nations Publications: UN Charter 1945 (**63** A); University of Exeter, Nazism 1919–1945 by J. Noakes and G. Pridham (**81** E, **85** A/C, **86** B/C/D); University of London: Britain's Economic and Social Development by R. Rundle (**43** B); Extract taken from Headline History by John Rae. Reproduced by kind permission of Unwin Hyman Ltd (**40** D, **60** B).

"Talking Atomic Blues" by Verne Partlow and Irving Bibo. 1958 Cromwell Music Ltd, Suite 207 Plaza 535, Kings Road, London SW10 0SZ. Copyright secured. All rights reserved. Used by permission (**60** E).

The Author and Publisher have made every attempt to contact copyright holders. They apologise for any unwitting infringement of copyright.